Published by Innovative Grammar

Lightning Source edition: April 2015

ISBN: 978-0-9838990-1-3

About the Authors

Janelle Cameron

Janelle is a language development and literacy consultant who works with K-12 teachers in California and across the southwestern United States to develop methods and skills for accelerating English language learning. Much of her work and academic research involves helping teachers and administrators to better understand English grammar and how to teach it to students in ways that are fun and motivating. She has a special interest in helping teachers to learn ways that can move "intermediate" students to levels of academic English competence necessary for content area studies. Janelle is co-author of a popular book on teaching English grammar concepts that are essential for academic reading and writing. She is director of project development for Innovative Grammar.

Kevin Clark

Kevin Clark is the senior consultant and founder of Clark Consulting and Training, Inc., a California-based organization that has provided services to schools, districts and states across the country since 1989. Much of his organization's work deals with the design, implementation, and measurement of instructional programs for English learners. He and his consulting team have assisted districts with programs ranging from late-exit bilingual to intensive structured English immersion. His company is located in Clovis, CA.

Innovative Grammar is a consortium of language teachers and researchers who exchange ideas, knowledge, and effective practices in the teaching of English grammar both to English learners and to English-only students.

Style Notes to Help the Reader

We make use of a couple of different text styles in this book to assist the reader to make sense of what may be new terminology or concepts. We also *don't* do some things in the quest for the same.

First, we use italics to refer to the proprietary methods we reference throughout the book. We do so to emphasize that clarity and accuracy of methods goes a long way in unifying instruction across a site or district. Because each method typically has some related support elements, we present those in bold text and in caps on their first reference. After that, we retain the capitals format but drop the bold. We present student voices in italics and try to avoid the bulky use of quotation marks.

Second, we abstain from over-citing every reference to a theory or generally known concept in the field of language teaching and learning. The citations contained herein should be sufficient for the reader desiring more information on a particular topic or idea. We used our best judgment in determining whether an idea is used with sufficient frequency as to no longer merit a full academic citation. This book is not a compilation of research nor a report on our own or anyone else's research; that is a book for a different day and probably a different audience. This book is for educators of the English language.

Introduction

Few issues are as challenging in public education today as those presented by students who lack full English proficiency. These students, numbering more than five million nationally, are distributed across all grades and in all states. Sometimes lost in these startling numbers are the English learners enrolled in secondary schools, defined as grades seven through 12. More than 1.5 million students identified as English learners nationally are attending junior and senior high schools. But as anyone familiar with secondary education would know, the 7-12 education world is about credits accumulation, prior academic knowledge, and English language mastery. Indeed, secondary education is about learning new ideas, concepts, themes, and curricular relationships through a language medium that is rarely acknowledged or discussed, but frequently taken for granted: English. More than ever before, secondary education is centered around students demonstrating their knowledge and their ability to analyze and synthesize in both written and spoken forms throughout all content areas. To do this, students must utilize the currency of the institution: English.

Tragically, and what gave rise to this book, is that the great majority of secondary English learners typically experience one of two extremes in their educational life. The first extreme is a conscious or unconscious denial by educators, board members, and the general public that they lack full English competence. Essentially, they are treated educationally as just another student and are enrolled in classes based on age or grade, given assignments, and awarded grades and credits on their way along a typical graduation track. Their English proficiency—or lack thereof—is not seen as a delimiting factor for their academic success, nor as a barrier to their full and robust participation in schooling. In the worst case, their lack of English competence is simply not acknowledged by the adults in charge. In the other case, their language shortcomings are trivialized.

For another group of English learners, the typical secondary treatment is at the other extreme. They are enrolled in one or more so-called English language development courses that frequently use low-level materials that lack focus and coherence. They may have a reading class that is designed to remedy their typical profile of reading three or more grades below grade-level. They could have courses titled *SDAIE Science*, or *ELD Social Science*, usually euphemisms for slower instruction that features little in the way of addressing what most bars them from meaningful academic participation: English. Throw in a study hall period for good measure or a class where they are a teacher's aide. It is not uncommon to find students in these settings who have been identified as English learners since elementary school. Most will "graduate" with about the same level of academic English competence as when they started secondary school. It is hardly surprising that secondary drop-out rates for English learners are staggering, though suspiciously under-reported, not reported, or not calculated.

What both of these approaches to dealing with the secondary English learner challenge have in common is that they deny—sometimes overtly and sometimes covertly—what these students need most to actually succeed in a secondary school setting. Well-intentioned counselors, school administrators, and teachers routinely do not openly or candidly discuss the common denominator among students that most persuasively explains poor reading comprehension, an inability to produce academic writing, poor grades, and stymied progress in mastering English. Sometimes trapped by ideology, walled in by tradition, or blinded by parochialism, educators tiptoe around what ails these young men and women. We state clearly the diagnosis here and throughout this book:

As a group, secondary English learners do not understand, use, control, or even know about the fundamental grammar rules of the English language that are requisite for academic achievement.

Secondary English learners are often the playground equivalent of *streetballers*, kids who have "figured out" basketball or soccer to the best of their ability and without instruction or coaching, but who lack a firm foundation in the fundamentals. They sometimes make a basket, they can dribble the ball slowly, they know the game's basic structure and know where to go whether they are on offense or defense. But they lack the game's underlying rules and skills to play organized ball successfully. Analogized to their schooling, they are *gisters;* they comprehend the essence of school lectures, textbooks, and themes, but when they are asked to convey, analyze, compare, contrast, synthesize, or evaluate the details of that knowledge by producing academic language—orally or in writing—their lack of fundamentals and advanced control is evident. This book is about addressing head-on the plight of secondary English learners and their teachers, who also share the frustration of knowing that what students most need is frequently what they get less of—focused, applicable, and engaging instruction in the logic, structure, and wonder of English language grammar.

We present here a *New View* of what English language development instruction for secondary English learners *could be, can be,* and *is* in a burgeoning number of schools and districts. Unabashedly and without apology, we argue for the provision of purposeful, intensive, and systematic teaching of English grammar skills to these students immediately. We look at schooling as a set of tasks that places certain linguistic demands on students. These linguistic demands assume that students have a sufficient grammar inventory to draw upon, and that they will make the correct choice. The underlying assumption, of course, is that English learners actually have an inventory of grammar knowledge and skills from which to choose. If grammar were a buffet line, most adolescent English learners have only been served a couple of basic entrées, a sparse salad, and maybe a vegetable or two. The metaphor is perhaps coarse, but accurate.

As English learners move from elementary settings to higher grade levels, the linguistic demands—and the corresponding language choices students must make—get increasingly more complex. Going back to the buffet metaphor, educators (read: teachers, schools, policy makers) expect English learners to present an expanded language buffet with more variety of entrées, greater and more sophisticated side dishes and desserts that wow their academic palates. As these students move up the ladder of grades, schooling gets harder, both linguistically and content-wise. Yet their linguistic inventories —the minimal food on their plate—frequently stay the same, fossilized as a function of repeated practice with few structures, no new structures being added, and a school system that trivializes language learning by assuming that sitting in class with an English-speaking teacher equals language learning. We argue—and demonstrate in this book—that when students know, understand, and control more English grammar structures and their uses, the more choices they have to meet the linguistic demands of school.

English learners need this knowledge of grammar and these skills today in order to understand their second-period math lecture, to read and comprehend a passage from *Uncle Tom's Cabin* in fourth period, and to write a convincing essay in sixth-period science about why certain chemicals should not be mixed together. We show in each chapter why grammar instruction is essential and foundational for the two main metrics of secondary school success: reading comprehension and academic writing. We lay out specific methods for teaching grammar that are engaging, interactive and that accelerate English proficiency in ways most educators never thought possible. We argue that parochial diagnoses commonly attributed to English learners — poor comprehension, auditory processing deficiencies, and fallacious or illogical thinking— have more to do with lack of familiarity with certain language structures and their use in academic settings than with cognitive demands or cognitive deficiencies.

In sum, this book shows a clear path to do what has needed to be done for these students for far too long. If we are going to ask secondary English learners to learn in English, then let's start by first teaching them English.

Kevin Clark & Janelle Cameron

Table of Contents

What does the research say on language teaching?

To say that the search for the *Holy Grail* of educational research is in full force in today's educational environment would perhaps be an understatement. Indeed, from university libraries to professional development rooms to school staff lounges across the country, the sometimes innocuous, sometimes venomous question "*But what does the research say?*" booms ominously. The question itself seems to suggest that there is a single source or compendium of veracity out there that renders some ideas good and others bad. If we just had that research, the script goes, we could get on with doing the right and best thing. While we are quick here to agree that research in and of itself is not a bad thing, we also point out that it frequently serves to either maintain a *status quo* ("Biff, settle down. This is research based.") or to polarize teachers ("Well, if you've got three studies that say Y is true, then we will find four studies that say X is truer.") rather than to foment innovative and effective practices. Why would we say this?

First, the question *What does the research say?* is itself somewhat silly for it implies that there is one unified tome of research that definitively solves all problems involving humans, teaching, and learning. There are vast differences in the both the interpretation and design of research studies. A phenomenological piece of research, for example, is quite different from a theoretical research study versus a quasi-experimental study. And true experimental studies, complete with control and experimental groups and randomized group assignment, are another very different type of research. So which is the correct one that we will use to rationalize, support, and defend our selection of methods for teaching English? Before we answer that, let's first consider the applicability of research findings.

When many educators ask for research, what they frequently desire is a definitive pronouncement of whether method X will work better than method Y in classroom Z on a given day in a school setting similar to their own. The reality is that most studies have limitations and delimitations, many of which are openly addressed by a study's author or authors in the preface to their findings. It is usually in the first pages that the authors also caution against over-generalization of their findings. One of the biggest limitations to a study is its generalizability. In other words, do the findings from the study seem to logically translate (read: generalize) to our issue at hand? Uninformed study-seekers tend to look for a study—or group of studies—that supports a very broad and difficult-to-research Gestalt that would have instant generalizability. So they ask a general question. For example, what if young parents looked for *the research* on spanking children. Could they dial up a study by asking this as their research question: *Is spanking our kids good for them*? As you can see, the inquiry is a bit broad. But educators ask such questions all the time: *What reading program is best? Does correcting students' errors help them? Is teaching spelling important?* These are wide-ranging topics—what true research people would call multivariate objects of study—that lend themselves to a whole lot of input factors, interpretations, and confounding variables. Good research has one major element to get right at the start: a very narrow research question.

Finally, correlation is not the same as causality. If a study suggests with some correlation co-efficient number, say .37, that allowing students to select their own writing prompt produced X number more words than when forced to write on a topic, we can get excited. Certainly, we might say, this means that we ought to let our students pick so that they will write more words. Not quite, for correlation merely suggests—with a varying amount of mathematically derived confidence—that these two things seem to move together or apart in some direction. But wouldn't causality be a beautiful thing in social science research? If you do A then B will happen. Now that is beautiful, but not what social science research produces in the overwhelming majority of cases. So be careful with correlation. And be careful about too much reliance on its doting parent, the Scientific Method. While science has given us much to think about and link to our practice (*praxis*), it must be remembered that the Scientific Method itself cannot be experimentally tested. That is a lot to think about the next time someone blithely asks...*So what does the research say*?

In answering this question, our approach is to list narrow questions (or at least as narrow as we can parse them) and to provide a cross-section of studies whose results support a particular treatment or approach. Is this summary exhaustive? No and of course not. This is not a research book, but we did want to provide some usable citations for those readers whose late-night academic curiosity can't be controlled. By saying all of this, we are of course acknowledging that there are contrary studies and that the studies we cite may not be anyone else's favorites. We provide here a condensed research summary of the main themes taken up in the pages ahead. In each of those sections is additional information particular or specific to that method.

1.   What is the current state of scientific research in the area of effective instruction for English learners?

Gersten and Baker (2000) set out to synthesize the research on effective instruction for English learners and were only able to locate five controlled intervention studies over a 20-year period. Similar conclusions about the state of scientific research in this field were echoed by August & Hakuta (1997) in their report entitled *Improving Schooling for Language-Minority Students: A Research Agenda*. They concluded that little scientific research had been conducted with school-age English learners, and expressed their concern about how "politics have constrained the development of sound practice and research in this field" (August & Hakuta, 1997, p. 148). Schleppgrell (2004) laments that although much research has focused on the features of early reading and writing in school contexts, less work has been done related to the kinds of tasks that challenge students in middle and high school classrooms.

Gersten and Baker (2000) noted that much of the research they located was qualitative case studies that drew inferences that did not seem supported by the data. A recent review of U.S.

research on ELLs conducted by Genesee, Lindholm-Leary, Saunders, & Christian (2004) found fewer than 50 studies that focused on English oral language outcomes and used sound methodology. They noted that only one study examined the effects of instruction on students' English oral language proficiency. They conclude there is little U.S. research literature to guide the design and delivery of oral ELD instruction or to substantiate its effects.

2.   *What empirical research supports the time-on-task principle and the allocation of time to discrete grammar skills instruction for English learners?*

Time as a critical instructional variable is a consistent theme throughout the research on student achievement, regardless of whether the findings are from studies comparing effective and ineffective teachers in the United States or from studies comparing the effectiveness of instruction in basic skills across different countries. Time-on-task has long been recognized as an important contributor to academic success because learning is partly a function of the time spent engaged in a task so that individual differences in time-on-task contribute to individual differences in academic skills (Bloom, 1974; Carroll, 1963). Specific research in this area related to English learners and the learning of English is relatively thin, possibly due to the fact that most states have no minutes requirement in their education codes for ELD, save for Arizona and Massachusetts. An internal three-year study completed by the Arizona Department of Education showed annual reclassification rates of more than 25 percent after the state moved to a daily four-hour block of grammar-based ELD instruction (Giovannone, 2011). Prior to 2009, there was no requirement for a certain number of ELD minutes in Arizona. During that period, average statewide annual reclassification rates never eclipsed eight percent (Santa Cruz, 2010).

Other studies that support the time-on-task to student achievement relationship are abundant. Borg (1980), in his summary of the research on the relationship between time and school learning, noted a consistent finding: "The amount of time that students are engaged in relevant reading and mathematics tasks is positively associated with academic achievement" (p. 59). Despite being somewhat difficult to operationalize, student engagement is recognized in the literature as an important link to student achievement and other learning outcomes (McGarity & Butts, 1984; Capie & Tobin, 1981; Fisher, Berliner, Filby, Marliave, Cahen, & Dishaw, 1980). Karweit (1983) reviewed time-on-task research over the last 50 years, noting that notwithstanding their methodological variances, these studies produce a positive association between time and learning.

3.   *What empirical research supports the need for allocating fixed periods of time to teaching certain elements of the English language?*

How teachers allocate time in classrooms has been the subject of extensive empirical research. In a comprehensive multi-year study of teaching practices, Fisher, et al (1980) found drastic differences in the amount of time teachers allocated to different skill areas, as did Rosenshine (1980). Berliner (1984), in a review of the research literature on teacher decisions and time allocations found wide variations among teachers for both content and time allocation decisions. Empirical research on this issue for school-age English language learners is almost non-existent. However, a study by Saunders, Foorman, & Carlson (2006) analyzed instructional practices and time allocations for English skills teaching in classrooms that had an identified ELD block, and classrooms that did not have such a block of time. They found that English learners in classrooms that had a separate ELD block had greater percentages of instructional time devoted to oral language and literacy activities than EL students in classrooms without a separate ELD block. ELL students in the separate-block configuration had modest but significantly higher English oral language and literacy scores on the Woodcock Language Proficiency Battery.

4. *What empirical research supports the explicit teaching of discrete English language skills?*

Ellis (2002) provided evidence from a variety of sources on the role of frequency in second language learning. He argued from the data that the abstraction of regularities within a complex language system is frequency based. He notes that for simple structures, minimal exposure may be enough. But for more complex or obscure structures, frequency may largely determine whether the form is acquired or not, in conjunction with learner's aptitude and the teacher's methodologies. Taraban (2004) found in an empirical study that learning certain grammatical conventions was greatly facilitated either by providing explicit instruction or by drawing learners' attention to the concept through the use of specific instructional approaches. Saunders, Foorman, & Carlson (2006) conducted research on the use of certain instructional elements in a reading program for ELLs, including an enhanced role for discrete language skills teaching. Students participating in the experimental group achieved significantly higher than ELL students in the control group (ES = 1.08). The intervention students made gains in English reading comprehension from more than 1 standard deviation below the normative sample to within the normal range (standard score = 98) at posttest. This contrasts with students in the control group, whose standard scores at pre-test were also low (82) and who made relatively little gain in reading comprehension in English (standard score = 84). From their meta-analysis of studies conducted during the past 20 years, Norris and Ortega (2000) concluded that focused second language instruction is more effective than implicit types and that instructional effects are durable over time. In one of the studies, Spada and Lightbown (1993) found that teachers who integrated grammar lessons into their communicative lessons were more effective than teachers who ignored grammar and those who only addressed it in decontextualized grammar lessons. Fotos and Ellis (1991) conducted experiments that asked students to solve grammar problems in the target language. They concluded that learners who are made aware of certain target structures in language are more likely to notice them than students who were not made aware of the target structures.

5. *What empirical research supports the teaching of discrete English language skills to English learners in a particular order?*

Some researchers have posited a "natural" order of acquisition common to all English learners regardless of age, learning environment, or prior languages learned (Dulay & Burt, 1973, 1974; Bailey, Madden, & Krashen, 1974). Brown (1973) presented empirical evidence of a similar order of acquisition of grammatical *functors*, setting in motion a series of studies which came to be known as the "morpheme order studies," all of which attempted to test several possible determinants of the order of functor acquisition (Brown, 1973, p. 379). Bailey, Madden, & Krashen (1974) found that the grammatical learning orders for Spanish and non-Spanish speakers were correlated (r=.926, p,<.005), and that the order for the adults in the study was extremely similar to the child order found earlier by Dulay and Burt (1973). Larsen-Freeman (1976) attempted to determine a single explanation for the order of grammatical acquisition, and tentatively concluded that the major cause of the order was the frequency of the input to the learner. Larsen-Freeman and Long (1991, p.91) have emphasized that, of all the determinants of acquisition order, "only input frequency has much empirical support to date." Goldschneider and DeKeyser (2005) conducted a meta-analysis that combined data from children and adults to determine how much of the total variance in English as a second language functor order can be accounted for by a combination of five factors: perceptual salience, semantic complexity, morphophonological regularity, syntactic category, and frequency. The researchers conclude that these five factors account for a large percentage of the variance in order of acquisition of grammatical structures, suggesting that "perceptual salience" (consciously noticing something, in this case, elements of grammar) is the ultimate predictor of the order of learning. Perceptual salience is a linguistics term, defined by the authors as the property of a structure that is perceptually distinct from other linguistic input. They suggest that a primary task of teachers is to make the functors more salient in an attempt to bring them to the learner's consciousness.

Defining Language for Instructional Purposes

Like so many aspects of life, one's definition of an object or idea frequently bears strong resemblance to how one interacts with that object or idea. If I define a computer as a magic box whose operation is one of mystery to me, my use of the computer is likely to reflect that definition. I hold it in awe, respect its miracle powers, but stand afar from using it myself because I have little understanding of how to make it serve me and my purposes. Doctors define the body in terms of organs, functions and systems, and much—if not all—of their methodology derives from that taxonomy. Using an example closer to teaching, if I define *reading* as an interpretive act largely influenced by one's life experiences (eisegesis), I will likely approach reading instruction along methodological lines consistent with my definition. By contrast, if my definition of reading is that it is the application of a series of individual micro skills utilized to determine the literal meaning of the words (exegesis), then my methods and assessment processes proceed from there. Language teaching is no different. Our definition of *language* drives our practices, even if we are not consciously aware of our definition.

It is paradoxical that so much verbal attention is placed on the materials and methods for teaching English to students and so little—if any—time is allocated to clearly defining what we mean by the word *language.* Definitions for language vary. Some argue that it is a socially constructed artifact used for conveying culture, while others identify language as a shared tool for communication, or as a semiotic system for learning social order, or simply something that humans do naturally. Many teachers were taught to define language in terms of acronyms like BICS (Basic Interpersonal Communication Skills) and CALP (Cognitive Academic Language Proficiency) (Cummins, 1991), recalling what was likely propagated during many hours of in-service, college instruction, or teacher certification programs. Unfortunately for English learners and for their teachers as well, none of the aforementioned "definitions" of language present educators with an actionable taxonomy that can be used for helping students to improve their English.

One could argue that loose definitions of the word *language* during the past three decades have served in large measure to trivialize language-teaching methodology. For example, if language learning is a natural and subconscious process, then my method of choice should logically be the *Natural Approach* (Terrell, 1991). If I believe that language is learned through the study of "modified" grade-level academic content areas like math, science, social science, and language arts, then I would blithely assume that SDAIE (Specially Designed Academic Instruction in English), or SIOP (Sheltered English Observation Protocol) (Echevarria, Short & Vogt, 2000) would do the trick. If I defined language as something that is learned subconsciously through simple exposure, I would sit an English learner next to a native English speaker and await the results.

In this book we define language by using a straightforward taxonomy that is both useful as a definition and as a compass for language teaching and assessment. As a bonus, this definition allows us to clearly define another pesky term–*English language development* (ELD). By operationalizing language in this way, many of the so-called "simple" language-teaching methods are quickly exposed for what they and their related definitions are: a trivialization of the algorithmic complexity of language and the hard work necessary to both teach and learn a new language to a level of academic competence. *Language is complicated and requires focused and sustained instruction, effort, and study to learn it.* So let's start by understanding a definition of language that will serve as our guide. It is the classical taxonomy that is used the world over to describe, analyze, and teach languages.

The Language Star:

A Useful Way to Define Language

There are five aspects of English—or any language, for that matter— that are important to understand. By seeing how each works in conjunction with the others, teachers can better understand how a particular method either addresses or does not address a student's particular language need. Conversely, by using the elements described here, we can discuss a student's strengths as well, thus forming a more complete profile of language competence.

The *Language Star* below shows each of the five elements of language. You will perhaps already be familiar with some of the terms.

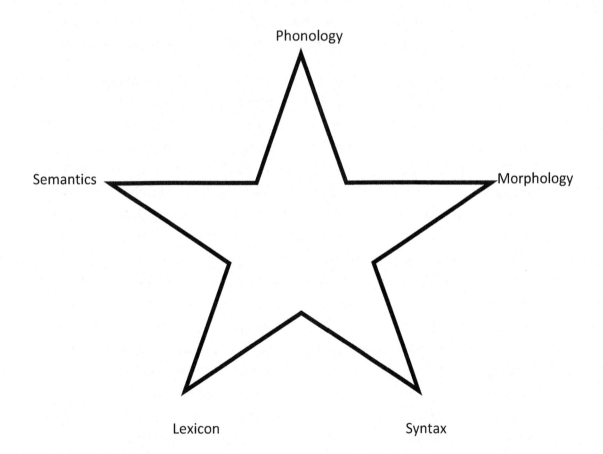

Phonology: This aspect of language is concerned with the smallest units of sound in a language. English has approximately 44 different sounds that are combined to form the words in the language. By contrast, the Spanish language has 24 sounds, or phonemes. On a practical level, phonology refers to a student's ability to actually produce each of these sounds, and to be able to hear these individual sounds. Phonological development is of vital importance for English learners, and largely untaught at any level. Without being able to hear the sounds or produce those sounds, it will be difficult to develop a base of understanding for the later development of graphophonics (letters and sounds) necessary for solid reading progress and spelling. Teachers have frequently assumed that students will develop an "ear" for language without direct instruction. Similarly, some theorists have argued that accent develops naturally; just sit English learners near native English speakers and all will resolve itself. Anyone who has ever tried to learn a foreign language knows that the phonological aspect can be daunting. It requires focused practice and attention to hear new things and to use the teeth, tongue, nose, throat, lips, diaphragm, and air to sound like a native speaker. Unfortunately, legions of English learners have carried poor accents and underdeveloped ears up the grade-level ladder, resulting in a host of issues that manifest themselves in academic settings: poor spelling, inability to take lecture notes, mispronunciation, hearing words incorrectly, and poor or no voice modulation when reading aloud, among many others. Sadly, many English learners fear speaking English aloud for lack of basic instruction and practice in English phonology.

Morphology: This is the study of the smallest units of meaningful sound in a language. This sounds tricky, but it's pretty simple. In other words, morphology is about the prefixes and suffixes—affixes taken together—that can change the meaning of a word. Described by way of rules, every morpheme is either a base or an affix. For example, say the word *cats*. How many separate "meaningful" sounds are there? Well, first there is the base word itself, *cat*. Then there is the morpheme *s*. So there are two morphemes in the word *cats*. Another important element of morphology is the range of word endings (inflections) used in English to represent verb tenses. By adding "ed" or "ing" to a base verb, we have changed the meaning of the word. Morphology can sometimes be tricky, so we will agree to define it like this: the various meaningful word parts, including verb inflections, which form the building blocks of our language. It becomes apparent in this discussion that English learners frequently lack direct instruction in how to change words to create different meanings. Further, most older English learners have received little instruction about how to identify a part of speech from a word's morphological characteristics. Moreover, the typical absence of sequenced verb tense teaching leaves many of these students with vastly underdeveloped knowledge of how to conjugate the many tenses of English. A glaring implication of underdeveloped verb tense knowledge is a key factor in poor reading comprehension. In short, a mastery of English morphology is not optional if our goal is to teach students to accurately command English for use in academic situations.

Syntax: This refers to the rules that govern the order of words in a language. English relies on several syntax rules. For instance, adjectives frequently come before nouns: *the red car.* Adjectives can also come after the verb *to be* and other linking verbs: *The tree is green.* Verbs tend to follow the subject of a sentence, while prepositions come before nouns. There are others, but the important thing to understand here is that, without these word order rules, learning new vocabulary, understanding complex oral language, and reading and writing will be extremely difficult, if not impossible. By way of analogy, learning long division is made much more difficult if one does not know the times tables. Similarly, solving an algebraic equation is greatly aided by following the mathematical order of operations rules.

A strong case can be made that syntax—word order rules— is and has been the most neglected element of English language teaching in classrooms over the past 30 years. Research on the human brain underscores the critically important role syntax development plays in not only language, but in reading comprehension, thinking skills, and writing proficiency. You will see in the methods section a rich variety of powerful and engaging syntax-building methods.

Lexicon: In technical terms, lexicon refers to the total stock of lexical items in a language. More simply, lexicon is the supply of words available to a person. For example, there is a lexicon of golf (bogey, birdie, flange, plumb-bob, hosel, divot, chip and run, etc.), which includes an entire word bank of phrases, nouns, and verbs that make sense only to other golfers. Likewise, teachers typically share a specialized lexicon; words that are meaningful to them in the context of teaching, but which may be incomprehensible or even unknown to non-educators. Many English learners have sizeable lexicons; they know a lot of words. Unfortunately, what is frequently lacking is how to use those words in a correctly structured sentence with the proper meaning and how to understand those words in written text. The other side of the coin is to be able to understand a word as it is used in a sentence spoken or written by someone else. It is not uncommon to see English learners writing and even memorizing long lists of words for which they do not know the meaning or how to use in a real sentence. Simply put: knowing a word is not the same as knowing when and how to use it and for what desired end or purpose.

Semantics: This is the study of word meanings. Together with lexicon, we could refer to these as "vocabulary"; knowing a word, its meaning, and how to use it in a sentence properly. The English language can be a semantic minefield for English learners, since so many words have multiple meanings and sometimes depend largely on other language elements for understanding. It frequently seems that just when we have taught our students what a word means, that word pops up in another sentence or context where it means something completely different. That is the wonderful—and sometimes whacky—world of semantics.

Still, students can see semantics as a fun exploration of the English language when it is viewed as one slice of language and not the end-all-be-all.

In conclusion, the categories described in this section form the internal components of the large system we call *language*. By having a working knowledge of these components, teachers can better understand how to plan and deliver instruction that focuses on one or more of these elements. By using the *Language Star* as an instructional compass, we can better guard against tilting our instruction too heavily in only one or two areas to the exclusion of others. Finally, to be considered truly competent in a language, one must demonstrate control of each element and use them collectively to receive and produce linguistic messages. This is the challenge that confronts our students and us.

Parts of Speech

Old Views

For some folks, the mere mention of *parts of speech* evokes a feeling of dread, tedium, and sometimes anger. Long-suppressed memories of learning dreary definitions for each part of speech come roaring back, sometimes followed by flashes of sentence diagramming and thick grammar books that went on and on with endless explanations and bland examples of what seemed like 888 parts of speech. Indeed, extreme forms of what we will call a *Classical View* of language endorse the notion that learning definitions and diagramming sentences would somehow be of benefit to the average student. In reality, those practices could seem horrifying to all but the most ardent lovers of taxonomies. For our purposes, the eight parts of speech will serve us well in our short exploration of three phases—or schools of thought—of language learning and teaching. We will call the first two phases the Old View, though with the benefit of hindsight they could not be more opposite. The third phase—the one advanced in this book—will be called the New View. Such an organizing system will begin each chapter to help the reader see how definitions of language and their related approaches to teaching and learning have impacted teachers and students.

Ready for a short story about the two lives of the Old View? We'll call the oldest one the Classical View, and the other simply the Old View. Both advanced precepts and practices about language teaching and learning that brought about in many cases very predictable and contradictory results. In short, the Classical View emphasized knowing about language and produced students who understood language structure but could not always use it. The second old view is what the majority of teachers have been taught, namely that language is naturally acquired in low-stress environments without direct instruction. Its outcome is the genesis of this book: thousands of English learners who have sat in English-speaking and so-called bilingual classrooms for multiple years but who arrive at secondary schools knowing little or nothing about the structure of English. They have limited linguistic inventories and cannot use grammar to assist them with reading comprehension and academic writing.

Let's dig a little deeper and see how the eight parts of speech fit or don't fit into these two old views and how they serve as the major stars of the New View. A couple of analogies will get us started. Imagine your kitchen having one single shelf or counter onto which all of your cooking utensils, pots, pans, mixes, flours, spices, and foods to be cooked were piled. As you set about making a dish, you would rummage through the mass of "kitchen stuff" looking for the correct pot, the necessary stirring device, and the various main ingredients and seasonings to be used. How frustrating would that be?

How about this example (and one that might be fairly accurate for some)? Have you ever seen an open garage door or closet that is packed to the gills with stuff piled high, sideways, items sticking out, a literal mound of unrelated items that seems ready to spill out with the removal of even one of the items? When new things arrive, they are added to the garage or closet based on the same system of simply throwing it into the mix, hoping it will stick and not fall or disturb any of the other items. What both of these scenarios show is lack of an organization system that specifies categories based on certain traits or features.

Maybe it wasn't either of these examples that lead Dionysius Thrax to be the individual seen as first responsible for dividing words into eight groups. In fact, Dionysius's book, *Techne Grammatike* (The Grammatical Art), first introduced the eight parts of speech in the second century B.C. Before that time, no classification system existed for the Greek language. His book became a standard textbook for centuries and anchored early curriculum for one of the seven liberal arts: grammar. Indeed,

the study of grammar was seen as a close cousin to mathematics and logic because of its structure and utility for creating meaning, and for those reasons was considered the first step (the first of the *arts*) in a liberal arts education. Grammar education, the reasoning went, was just good mind training for the other arts that would follow in the totality of the liberal arts curriculum.

Thrax's life achievement was the development of a basic taxonomy of language—a classification system—which has yet to be replaced or improved in any major way. And this is why instruction in the parts of speech was a component of most U.S. public education classrooms through the 1960s. Not because of Thrax *per se*, but because educators around the world saw the ability to describe and classify the parts of language as a necessary ingredient for being skilled in the arts of language. For the Classical View, the study and analysis of the eight parts of speech was the epicenter of language teaching and learning. Even today, this component of the Classical View of language learning and teaching endures around the world.

Then a strange thing came to pass. The classifications that had survived and been taught for more than 18 centuries came to be vilified as boring, unnecessary, tedious, anathema to creativity and even racially discriminatory. Beginning in the 1950s, the first signs of what was then seen as an enlightened view of language learning and teaching began to emerge. Contemporary linguists of the time asserted that knowing and understanding the eight parts of speech was obsolete. Leading the charge was Charles Fries, a respected linguist who advocated for the use of scientific methods by linguists. His most influential work, *The Structure of English* (1952), presented a criticism of traditional grammar that was later relied upon by the National Council of Teachers of English (NCTE) for their frequent criticisms of U.S. public school grammar instruction.

The NCTE's main assertion was that teaching grammar hurt composition. As described by David Mulroy in his provocative book, *The War Against Grammar* (2003), the NCTE adopted in 1985 a formal resolution calling for class time at all grade levels to be devoted not to grammar teaching, but rather to opportunities for meaningful listening, speaking, reading, and writing. They also argued for ending testing practices that encouraged the teaching of grammar in lieu of those that measured improvements in writing. Grammar and its teaching, experts claimed, was simply and normatively bad. Paradoxically, modern dictionaries continue to list words according to their part of speech.

At this point in our story, the Classical View and its reliance on structure and nomenclature, took a beating. It was replaced in teacher education and liberal arts curricula by a different view of language teaching and learning that eschewed labeling and knowing parts of

speech. The 1900-year-old view that grammar instruction was useful and that knowing about the eight parts of speech was time well spent pretty much lost support in the United States in less than 30 years, from 1960-1990. Learning parts of speech, grammar rules, and their critical role in crafting polished communication just seemed too difficult.

So universities cut back on grammar courses as part of a liberal arts education, teachers new to the field entered classrooms with a different definition of language (i.e., *something humans do naturally to communicate*), and local and state boards of education started to adopt instructional materials that featured less or no grammar. For their part, many professors cranked out opinion pieces and theoretical studies masked as *research* proving that students could acquire English easily, at their own pace and without a teacher actually teaching language. After all, the enlightened team argued, we all mastered English and know nothing of its structure. Learning a second language is just as easy: stay calm, enjoy life and let the language sink in through osmosis.

And thus the Classical View of language learning and teaching, with its parts of speech and sterile rules of grammar, was replaced by what was then seen as a *New View*—students acquire language when they are relaxed and when the teacher provides them with understandable content area instruction with no focus on the language itself. By the mid 1980s, this view was firmly entrenched in teacher education and certification programs as the "right" way to help English learners *to acquire* English. Gone were the eight parts of speech and with them the grammar rules that governed their operation.

But almost five decades later, the precepts and practices of this enlightened view are largely responsible for the very condition we stated in the first pages:

As a group, secondary English learners do not understand, control, use or even know about the fundamental grammar rules of the English language that are requisite for academic achievement.

New View

The New View, as we define it in this book, is actually the best of the two Old Views with more emphasis on application for the purposes of reading comprehension and academic writing. In short form, the New View has these precepts:

1. Grammar, a system that uses the eight parts of speech as its input, is a classification system that allows language to be used, understood, and discussed. No matter how intuitively you understand space, you will not get far as an astronomer without knowing the differences between stars, planets, solar systems, and galaxies. In short, a detailed study of most anything begins by identifying, naming, and classifying its parts. We can thank our science teachers for not giving up on these ideas.

2. Aristotle explains the second precept: truth and falsehood can be attributed only to words organized by the rules of grammar into subjects and predicates (Ackrill, 1988). The meaning of sentences is created—in large and small part—by the rules of grammar.

3. It is near impossible to teach a subject that lacks terms for its parts and their relationships.

4. Producing language is the hallmark of language competence. Understanding someone else's sentences is useful, but understanding grammar allows one to create sentences that express one's original intent, and to better understand messages from others.

5. Grammar assists greatly in determining literal, or exact, meaning of spoken and written communication. By analyzing language for its literality, we can better understand and appreciate its figurative qualities.

Reading Comprehension Connection

Grammar is a wondrous tool for making sense of the written word. Though many people are not conscious of how they use their grammar to "make meaning" from text, for students not instructed in English grammar, the opposite is almost always true: they do not know enough about grammar or how it works to use it as a tool for comprehending text. The net result in too many cases is low or no reading comprehension. Let's be mathematical for a moment and look at something that we will call the *Comprehension Equation*. You will remember its parts because they are the same aspects of language to which all of the methods in this book are geared to teach. Here's a hint: it shines from the north. Yes, it's the *Language Star* and each of its points names a different aspect of language: *phonology, morphology, syntax, lexicon,* and *semantics*. For a quick refresher, take a minute to review these terms in the first part of this book. Now to the math part:

Comprehension = Phonology   Morphology   Syntax   Lexicon   Semantics

The *Comprehension Equation* holds that language comprehension, whether receptive or productive, is a function of these five elements. Keep thinking about math for a moment and try to figure out which mathematical operation would work best in the boxes between each term to make the equation true. In other words, is language comprehension like an addition (+) problem, wherein you simply add the values of each language aspect and the result is comprehension? (If comprehension equals 100, then each of the five aspects represents a number and together they sum to 100). Or is it an unwieldy combination of adding and subtracting and dividing? It's actually none of these. Here is the *Comprehension Equation* in its true and beautiful mathematical form:

Comprehension = Phonology X Morphology X Syntax X Lexicon X Semantics

Because it is a multiplication equation, If one of the aspects (morphology, syntax, lexicon, etc.) has a value of zero (as in, a student has no knowledge, understanding or control of that element), then comprehension can go to zero, as in zilch, nothing, *nada*. The theme of this chapter —the rationale, development and use of a *Grammar Wall*—clearly addresses the Syntax element of the *Comprehension Equation*. By understanding the parts of the language system (read: eight parts of speech) and understanding the rules that govern their order and function, students can use grammar as a foundational component and tool for reading with comprehension.

Academic Writing Connection

*I like this book. This book is a fun book. My friend has this book. He likes this book.
Books are good and fun.*

Most teachers and lay people alike would agree that the writing sample above hardly comports with any of the qualities of what might be called "academic" writing. By way of analysis, the sentences are short, they present a single tense, the verb is usually the second or third word, the syntax pattern is redundant, and each sentence starts with either a pronoun (*I, My, He*), an adjective (*This*), or a noun (*Books*).   The sentences are just boring. Unfortunately, there are thousands of similar writing samples posted on classroom walls around the country, testimonials to the naked fact that lack of knowledge about the parts of language and the rules that govern their relationships dooms too many students to simple writing patterns.

So what is *academic writing*? At the risk of offending learned academics, staff-lounge linguists, and Professor Higgins himself, academic writing means composing long sentences that feature a variety of grammar parts and rules.   Academic writing is about using more of the pieces of the language system and its rules to make longer, more information-packed sentences that sound different and more flavorful than the preceding sentences. And here is a secret kept from all English learners: *as you move up through the grades, the authors of your books use more and more of the available parts and rules in the sentences they write.* Not surprisingly, the average number of words per sentence in academic texts increases as a function of grade level, starting at around eight words per sentence in kindergarten and rising to sometimes more than 34 words per sentence in secondary school texts. Look at your own books through grammar eyes and you will see the same phenomenon. Authors write longer sentences by using more of the parts and more of the rules. What they don't do—different from English learners—is gain sentence length through the use of the word *and*, a popular writing device among grammar-impoverished English learners. Here is an example of how the simple conjunction *and* is relied upon by this junior high school-age English learner.

Science is a good subject and it is helpful to people and they study it to learn about plants and to learn about animals and how to use science to make things good for everyone.

Stitching short sentences together with low-level conjunctions is not academic writing under any scenario. Rather, it is compelling evidence for blocking out some space in your classroom to begin building a living, breathing, taxonomy-revealing *Grammar Wall*.   Let's get started!

 *Resource*

Grammar Wall

Description

The *Grammar Wall* is a physical language resource permanently posted in the language classroom. With a designated area for each part of speech, students and teachers refer to the wall to both correctly categorize and use language.

Purpose

This living language resource allows students to visually categorize parts of speech. The wall not only shows examples of each part of speech, but also provides clues that enable students to appropriately identify and use unfamiliar words based on their knowledge of morphology and syntax. As students advance in their language proficiency, the *Grammar Wall* serves as a tool to both reflect recently acquired words and to introduce new vocabulary.

Materials Needed

- ☐ adequate wall space (5x7 feet recommended)
- ☐ parts of speech placards
- ☐ sub-category headings
- ☐ index cards or pre-cut strips of paper
- ☐ markers

How to Build a *Grammar Wall*

While no two *Grammar Walls* are exactly the same, each should use the same framework to ensure that the tool is as useful as possible. Below are the steps for building a *Grammar Wall* and tips on how and where to get started.

Steps:

1. Make some room!
2. Arrange eight parts of speech.
3. Post placards.
4. Post sub-categories.
5. Post interrogatives.
6. Add words.
7. Use the wall.
8. Post syntax rules.
9. Post common endings.

Step 1-Make some room!

To have an effective *Grammar Wall*, it must be placed in a location that will allow students to interact with it. Every student in the room must be able to see the words on the *Grammar Wall* from wherever he or she is seated. The wall must also be large enough to accommodate at least 200 words. A minimum size of seven feet wide and five feet high is recommended.

Once the space for the wall has been acquired, it should be marked off in some way to distinguish it from the rest of the classroom. Consider using butcher paper for a background, borders, or even electrical tape or yarn to delineate each part of speech.

Step 2- Arrange space for each part of speech.

The parts of speech are to be placed in the following order: adjective, noun, pronoun, verb, adverb, preposition, conjunction, interjection. The parts of speech can be arranged horizontally in a line or with four on top and four below so long as the prescribed order is maintained.

Ensure that the parts of speech are clearly distinguishable from each other. Use tape, yarn, or different colors to differentiate parts of speech.

Tip!

The order matters!
The *Grammar Wall* is not posted in a haphazard manner. Rather, the prescribed order shows the order of a basic sentence. Think of a simple sentence: *The student learns.* Now consider the order: adjective (article), noun, verb. (Just like the *Grammar Wall!*)

Likewise, the lower level of the *Grammar Wall* houses the details of the sentence: *The student learns quickly (adverb) at school (prepositional phrase) because (conjunction) she is determined.*

Adjective

An adjective is a word that describes a noun or pronoun telling which one, how many, or what kind.

Step 3- Post parts of speech placards.

Each part of speech section should be marked by a placard that includes the title and definition. An example of a placard on the *Grammar Wall* is shown to the left. Note that the prominent title takes up almost half of the placard.

Simple definitions for each part of speech that can be used on the placards are provided on the following page.

Part of Speech	Definition	Examples
Adjective	An adjective is a word that describes a noun or pronoun, telling which one, how many, or what kind.	this, those, green, tiny, Italian, some, third, metallic, interesting
Noun	A noun is a word that names a person, place, thing, or idea. It can act or be acted upon.	Roger, priest, bowlers, the Golden Gate Bridge, tower, suitcase, council, flour, triangle, strength, neighborhood
Pronoun	A pronoun is a word that is used in place of a noun.	I, you, he, they, them, our, ours, herself, which, that, whose
Verb	A verb is a word that shows physical or mental action, being, or state of being.	to sway, to imagine, to remain, to seem, to appear, to attack
Adverb	An adverb is a word that is used to describe a verb, adjective, or another adverb telling how, where, or when.	slowly, thoughtfully, well, north, frequently, soon, extremely
Preposition	A preposition is a word that is used to show the relationship of a noun or a pronoun to another word.	under, before, of, into, around, like, with
Conjunction	A conjunction is a word that is used to join words of groups of words.	because, and, or, but, yet, when, while, if
Interjection.	An interjection is a word that is used alone to express strong emotion.	Wow! Yikes! Hooray!

Step 4- Post sub-categories.

To make the *Grammar Wall* more useful, the words should be categorized within their parts of speech. *Knowing the sub-categories for each part of speech assists students in accurately using unfamiliar words.* On the following page is a list of possible sub-categories for the parts of speech. Only use the sub-categories that either have previously been taught or will be taught during your language lessons.

When first building a *Grammar Wall,* it is helpful to post all of the sub-categories that will be taught throughout the year to assure that there is sufficient space.

> **Tip!**
> **Still not sure which categories to post?**
> The key question to ask is: "What would be useful for this group of students?"
>
> Beginning language students would not need collective nouns on the wall at first, while advanced students should no longer need singular and plural nouns posted.

Parts of Speech

Adjective	Noun
• Comparative/superlative • Articles • Demonstrative *Clauses • Number • Observation/quality • Size • Shape • Age • Color • Origin • Material • Qualifier	• Person, place, thing, idea (abstract) • Singular/plural • Irregular plural • Collective • Proper • Possessive • Non-count • Gerunds
Pronoun	**Verb**
• Personal subject • Personal object • Possessive • Demonstrative • Relative • Indefinite • Reflexive • Interrogative • Reciprocal	• Physical Action • Mental Action • Linking • Helping/Modals • Irregular • Phrasal
Adverb	**Preposition**
• Manner *Clauses • Direction • Frequency • Time • Intensity/Degree	• Time *Phrases • Location • Purpose • Relation
Conjunction	**Interjection**
• Coordinating • Subordinating (time, cause, condition, contrast) • Correlative	

28

Once the sub-categories for the *Grammar Wall* have been chosen, post them on the appropriate section of the wall. The categories should stand out from the sample words. Consider using index cards of a different color. Below is an example of what the section for adverbs would look like for a class that will learn all five sub-categories.

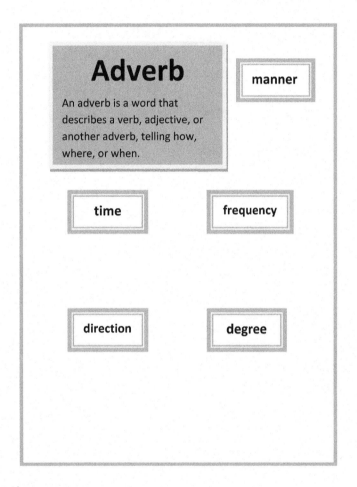

Step 5- Add interrogatives.

Regardless of grade or language level, most students are more familiar with the interrogatives: *who, what, where, when, why*, and *how* than they are with the terms for parts of speech. Adding the interrogatives to the *Grammar Wall* to indicate which question the words answer helps students understand how the parts of speech are to be used in writing and understood in sentences.

Each of the interrogatives can be answered by one part of speech or more. Write these interrogatives on index cards or sticky notes and attach them to the *Grammar Wall*. These interrogatives should be prominent as students will likely look for the interrogatives before the part of speech to which it is attached. The table on the next page shows where the interrogatives should be posted.

Adjectives *Who*	Nouns (subject) *Who*	Pronouns (subject) *Who*	Verbs *What*
(used to describe nouns and pronouns)			
Adverbs *How*	Prepositions *Why*	Conjunctions	Interjections
of manner	of purpose	*When* of time *Why* of cause	*Wow!*
Where of direction *When* of time/ frequency	*Where* of location *When* of time		

While the above shows which interrogatives should be posted and where, the example below shows how one section of the *Grammar Wall* would look with interrogatives and sample words.

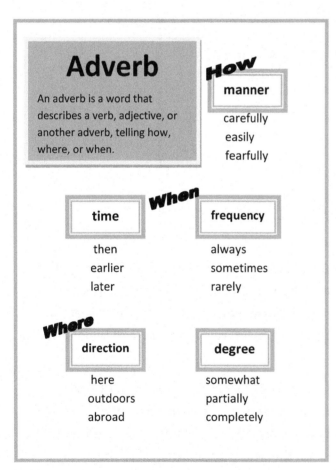

Tip!
Remember the prescribed order for parts of speech on the *Grammar Wall*?

Attaching the interrogatives to the *Grammar Wall* further reinforces the difference in complexity between the two levels. Note that the top row, the first four parts of speech, only answer the "who" and the "what" to form a basic sentence while the bottom row answers all of the detail questions.

Step 6- Add words!

Words are the most important component of the *Grammar Wall*. With the placards, sub-categories, and interrogatives placed, words are now needed to complete the wall. If certain parts of speech have been instructed in previous language courses, words can be placed under the appropriate sub-categories as examples. If a sub-category is new, wait until it is taught to introduce example words.

> ***Tip!***
> **Verbs in the Infinitive Form**
> Verbs *must* be posted in the infinitive form (to + base verb = to run, to see, to believe) for two important reasons.
> 1. Students can conjugate the verb to any verb tense.
> 2. Infinitive verbs distinguish the word as a verb rather than another part of speech (e.g. "to look" (verb) v. "the look" (noun)).

To teach a new sub-category to students, start with the placard and definition of the part of speech. Once students have understood the qualities of the main part of speech, introduce the sub-category. Teach the syntax rule for that part of speech (Syntax rules follow.) and allow students to practice using the new sub-category by providing sample words. Ask students if they can think of other words that would fit in the same category.

> ***Example***
> To teach adverbs of time: "Adverbs are words that describe verbs, adjectives, or other adverbs telling how, where, or when. Today we are going to learn about a type of adverb that describes verbs telling time. These adverbs answer the question 'when?'" We attach these adverbs to other verbs. For example, 'She will swim *soon.*' Can we attach these other adverbs of time to a verb to tell when? We will try the following adverbs together: later, then, now, today, tomorrow, yesterday."

Step 7- **Use** the *Grammar Wall*

The *Grammar Wall* can and should be used in every language lesson. Every method presented in this book refers to use of the *Grammar Wall.* Consider the following ten ways to use the *Grammar Wall.*

Ten Quick Ways to Use the Grammar Wall

1. *Verb Tense Study* sentence extenders. "Add a 'when' to your sentence."
2. *Four-Picture Story Frames* clues.
3. *Morph House* parts of speech identification
4. *Syntax Surgery* clues
5. Post words from *Syntax Surgery*
6. *Grammar Wall* games
7. Classify vocabulary or spelling words by part of speech.
8. Assign a part of speech to a student or group of students and have them add another word.
9. Assign a sentence formula (adjective+noun+verb+adverb+preposition+noun) and have students write sentences using only words from the *Grammar Wall.* (Red balloons float gracefully above clouds.)
10. Take all the words down and have students put them back in the correct spot after justifying their placement.

Step 8- Add syntax rules.

Once the basics of the *Grammar Wall* have been established, syntax rules can be added to further assist students in using the posted words. Near each part of speech, post the appropriate syntax rules. Twelve basic syntax rules are shown on the next page. Use sentence strips or something similar to add these rules to the *Grammar Wall*. The illustration below shows what a section of the *Grammar Wall* with syntax rules would look like.

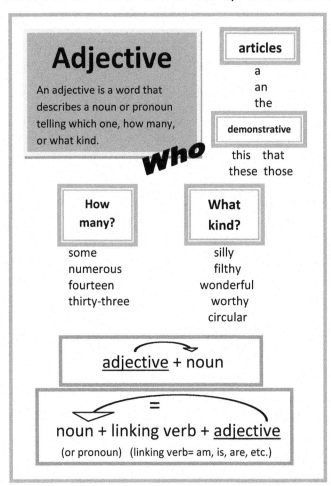

Tip!
Use removable tape or push pins to post the syntax rules. They can also be used with *Syntax Surgery*, *Morph House* and to assist students in writing sentences with correct syntax.

Basic Syntax Rules

1.	Subject + verb. noun pronoun	He walks.
2.	adjective + noun	The red ball
3.	= noun + linking verb + adjective (or pronoun) (linking verb= am, is, are, etc.)	The ball is red.
4.	noun ⟺ pronoun	(Pronoun replaces noun after noun is introduced.)
5.	preposition + noun (= prepositional phrase)	under the bridge
6.	**OR** adverb + verb + adverb	quietly reads **or** reads quietly
7.	Clause + conjunction + clause. (subject + verb) (subject + verb)	The students must stay inside because it is raining.
8.	Conjunction + clause, clause. (subject + verb) (subject + verb)	Because it is raining, the students must stay inside.
9.	verb + noun (transitive verb) (direct object)	Throw the ball.
10.	= noun + linking verb + noun (or pronoun) (to be verbs, to seem, etc.)	Whales are mammals.
11.	Noun + linking verb + prepositional phrase. (or pronoun) (to be verbs, to seem, etc.)	Squirrels were in the tree.
12.	_____ + coordinating conjunction + _____ (Can join **nouns, pronouns, verbs, prepositions, adjectives, adverbs**)	chocolate or vanilla

Step 9- Add common endings.

 Common word endings are also a helpful tool in assisting students in identifying parts of speech. Post some of the most common morphological endings to adjectives, nouns, verbs, and adverbs on the *Grammar Wall* and continue to add more as they are encountered throughout text. These endings can be displayed on their own chart or on vertical sentence strips next to the respective part of speech as shown in the illustration below.

Common Endings			
adjectives	**nouns**	**verbs**	**adverbs**
• able	• tion	• ing	• ly
• ive	• ence/ance	• ed	
• ic	• y	• s/es	
• y	• ing		
• ing	• al		
• ed	• ment		
	• ness		
	• er/or		

More important than a *Grammar Wall* with each of the additions listed in this chapter is that the *Grammar Wall* is used by both students and the teacher. Introduce the *Grammar Wall*, add some words, and get going! You will quickly see how useful it is.

What this Resource *Isn't*

It's <u>not</u> static wallpaper. The *Grammar Wall* is meant to be used and updated frequently. Other resources are not to be posted on it.

It's <u>not</u> optional. To complete the other methods in this book, the *Grammar Wall* is a necessary tool.

It's <u>not</u> a teaching method. The *Grammar Wall* is added to and used as a resource for other lessons.

It's <u>not</u> hidden. The *Grammar Wall* is only useful if it can be seen and accessed by the students.

Things to Re-think

1. Is it possible that many people came to dislike parts of speech and grammar because they could never see the rules? Wasn't everything just memorization of some invisible system?
2. If you walked into an artist's studio you would see brushes, easels, paper and other tools of that endeavor. What would you see in an auto shop? What tools are evident in most language-teaching classrooms?
3. Do you agree that the *Grammar Wall* shows students the chassis of language: nouns, pronouns, and verbs, and then lets them in on the secret that all of the other parts are just bolt-on accessories to the main grammar chassis?
4. How many analogous tools to the *Grammar Wall* can you think of from other disciplines, careers, tasks, or life? Hint: the table of periodic elements, a number line, a garage peg board...
5. How much grammar learning have all the Michael Jordan posters hanging in secondary language classes really accounted for? What's on your walls?

Administrators' Corner

<u>What to look for in a *Grammar Wall*:</u>

→ Is the *Grammar Wall* clearly labeled?

→ Is there sufficient space allotted? A minimum of 7'x 5' is recommended.

→ Are there words posted?

→ Are the words updated on a regular basis? Weekly?

→ Is the *Grammar Wall* labeled with the interrogatives?

→ Are there sub-categories appropriate to the language level of the class posted?

→ Do students make a habit of using the *Grammar Wall*?

→ Are words legible?

→ Are words written on paper of the same color and size?

→ Do the words posted reflect what is being taught in the classroom?

→ Are the posted words appropriate for the language level? Are they too simple? Too advanced?

What to Expect

➤ An initial hassle is figuring out where to find the required real estate in your classroom for the *Grammar Wall*. Remember: fight your desire to make it small. Fight your desire to hide it somewhere. Fight your desire to make up your own definitions for the parts of speech. Fight your desire to start building a *Grammar Wall* "next year."

➤ Secondary students will sometimes remark that such an ostentatious display of anything smacks of their elementary classrooms. Patiently explain that you have found an indispensible tool for their learning and will share it with them daily.

➤ Be prepared for students to make LOTS of connections between previously unrelated grammar information swimming around in their heads un-collated, uncollected, and uncategorized. The better your questions and displayed thinking, the better their connections and displayed thought will be.

➤ The *Grammar Wall* is an unapologetic attempt to make the messy clean. The most ornery, hard-to-handle words can find a home on a well-constructed and utilized Grammar Wall. You will hear the following many times when you slot a previously savage word into a neat and sanitary category with an explanation and rule/s for its use: *Ohhhh…*

➤ Consider investing in heating pads—for the necks of students who will constantly turn their heads to consult a living, breathing, taxonomy-revealing tool like the *Grammar Wall*. Encourage them to keep looking and learning.

Voices from the Classroom

The Grammar Wall is such an integral and beneficial component of teaching English Language learners. Not only does it help them identify parts of speech and organize basic syntax patterns, but it also provides an accessible resource. Placing words on the grammar wall that were new to students or out of their comfort zone allowed me as a teacher to use it as a reference to guide their vocabulary in writing and provided the students with an opportunity to incorporate more academic language into their writing. –Diane from Fresno, CA

Conversation and Content Area Vocabulary Methods

- *Language Warm-up*

- *Function Junction*

- *This or That*

- *Vocabulary Frames*

- *Vertical Sentence*

- *Morph House*

What empirical research supports the explicit teaching of phonology to English learners?

Several empirical studies have presented evidence that phonological awareness transfers from children's first language to their second (Bruck & Genessee, 1995; Cisero & Royer, 1995; Durgunoglu, Nagy, & Hancin-Bhatt, 1993; Geva & Siegel, 2000; Verhoeven, 1994). Chiappe, Siegel, and Gottardo (2002) found that kindergarten English language learners performed more poorly on measures of phonological awareness in English than native English speakers of the same age. Similar to other studies, Chiappe and Siegel (1999) found a clear link between phonological awareness and reading acquisition in Punjabi-speaking children learning to reading in English. The importance of phonological processing in the acquisition of reading has been found to be important (Catts et al., 1999; Siegel, 1993). Gottardo et al (1996) linked deficits in phonological processing and sensitivity in children to the development of syntactic skills. Couper (2006) tried to determine the effect of instruction on specific English pronunciation aspects and to see if gains were retained over time and integrated into phonological competence. Students received direct instruction in two specific areas of phonology. He reported decreases in error rates from 19.9% to 5.5% for the experimental group in the immediate post-test, compared to a control group of similar students who did not receive the explicit phonology instruction. The author noted gains were reported even for students who were identified to have fossilized phonological interlanguage characteristics (interlanguage refers to the use of more than one language system to create a hybrid language, sometimes referred to as Pidgin language). Perlmutter (1989) found improved intelligibility in older ESL learners during six months of language instruction that emphasized pronunciation. Derwing, Munro, and Wiebe (1997) similarly showed that students' long-term pronunciation improved significantly in a 12-week program emphasizing global production skills. They found that speakers who had instruction emphasizing certain prosodic features such as rhythm, intonation and stress could transfer their learning to spontaneous language production tasks. Their study also showed that certain instructional approaches in pronunciation enhanced students' oral production in three areas—comprehensibility, accent, and fluency.

What empirical research supports the explicit teaching of English oral language skills?

There is some evidence that measures of oral proficiency that index academic language use correlate positively with other measures of academic achievement (Genesee et al., 2004). At least one longitudinal study has suggested that preschool and kindergarten instruction that introduces elements of academic language use predicts subsequent literacy success in middle school (Dickinson & Sprague, 2001). Long-term studies of reading development by Catts, Hogan, and Adlof (2005) showed that, although listening comprehension predicts a relatively small amount of unique variance in reading scores for second graders, by fourth grade it uniquely predicts 21% of the variance, and by eighth grade, it uniquely predicts 36%. They noted similar findings for ELLs as reported by Hoover and Gough (1990). Munro and Derwing (1994) also conducted studies showing that accent can be detected by native speakers and that deliberate work to improve a speaking accent produces learner improvement.

What empirical research supports the explicit teaching of grammar related to language functions?

Students' difficulties in "reasoning," for example, may have more to do with their lack of familiarity with the linguistic properties of the language through which the reasoning is to be communicated rather than with students' cognitive deficiencies or the difficulty of the cognitive tasks involved. Students' use of linguistic styles that are conversational to present information in schooling contexts can be judged to be illogical or disorganized in their thinking (Clark, 1977). Judgments about students' abilities—right or wrong—are frequently based on how they express their knowledge.

An iconic linguistic demand—language function—made in schooling contexts is the request for definitions. Researchers have studied how some students' early childhood experiences prepare them for the "definitions game" that is played at school. The development of certain kinds of grammatical resources at home equips the child to use particular ways of reasoning by way of specific language structures, i.e., syllogisms. These same linguistically prepared students know how to sound authoritative, describe an event to someone who was not there or give directions for making something to someone with no prior knowledge. Snow, Cancini, Gonzalez, and Shriberg (1989), for example, observed that teachers often request definitions from students during lessons, then move to co-construction with the whole class of an acceptable common version. They also found that the most popular vocabulary "teaching" device in second through seventh grades rooms was the provision by the teacher of a list of words that students had to look up and copy the definitions from the dictionary. Giving definitions is an important way of using language at school and one way to demonstrate intelligence. Definitions that are valued by teachers seem to emphasize clear meaning and use of the word under study. Informal definitions frequently describe the speaker's relation to the item, i.e., *We have a hammer at home. It is my dad's*. Snow (1989) found that some children treated a request for a definition as a school task, giving well-planned, lexically specific information about the word without using personal information or sounding conversational. Snow et al (1989) also found that formal skill in defining words correlated positively with reading scores on standardized tests, while conversational style responses correlated negatively with those test results.

What empirical research supports the explicit teaching of English language vocabulary to English learners?

English vocabulary has historically occupied a central place in both literacy and content-area assessments and constitutes the most pervasive factor in U.S. intelligence tests (Wahlberg, 1989) Beck, McKeown, and Kucan (2002), Fitzgerald (1995a), Gersten and Baker (2000), Snow et al., (1998), and Ulanoff and Pucci (1999) all describe experimental results supporting the centrality of vocabulary in the comprehension of language-related tasks. Saunders, Foorman, & Carlson (2006) conducted research in the classrooms of 1,237 kindergarten EL students in three types of classrooms: immersion, dual immersion and transitional and found that explicit vocabulary instruction constituted an average of less than five percent of literacy-related instruction. August et al (2005) emphasize the critical nature of vocabulary teaching for English learners by citing research linking vocabulary development to reading proficiency.

Sounds of the English Language

Old View

Most people are flummoxed when asked to say how they developed their "native-like accent." "I don't know," they say. "This is how I have always talked." By contrast, most adults who have ever tried to learn a new language have found the pronunciation of the new language to be one of the most challenging tasks. Conversely, teachers and other folks are likely to marvel at how seemingly quickly young children "pick up" a native-like accent, but are surprised to learn that Mel Gibson actually has a recognizable Aussie accent that is quite different from the English he speaks while playing a New York movie cop. And speaking of famous characters, how did Eliza Doolittle finally pronounce correctly that most famous of language drills, *The rain in Spain stays mainly in the plain*?

Like so many elements of language learning and teaching, the subject of phonology—the sounds of a language—has at least two sides. Let's take a look.

One of the most parochial of assumptions about language learning—even for young children—is that they will just "pick up" how to pronounce the words and sentences of a new language. This Old View holds that non-native English-speaking children listen to others and after a while begin trying to

make the same sounds and words. With encouragement from adults, peers, and maybe even Sponge Bob, they gradually—or quickly—master the accent. While this seems to have some veracity for children learning a first language in a home setting, generalizing it to second language learning in a school setting has dangerous and predictable consequences. The Old View theory, though, is enticing in its simplicity: expose students to the new language in a low-stress environment and the native-like accent will follow in due time (however long that is, no one can say). The role played by a parent or caretaker in the home is now transferred to the teacher and English-speaking classmates and—voila! —perfect English pronunciation is the outcome.

Most teachers have been taught the following about how English learners of all ages will come to hear and say the sounds of the English language correctly.

- Students need to listen to the new language (English, in our case) for an indeterminate period of time.

- During this *Silent Period*, they should not be asked nor forced to produce oral language.

- As they interact with native speakers of English, they will hear and begin to differentiate between sounds.

- When they are ready, they will start speaking. Their accent will improve as they continue to listen and speak the new language.

- No effort need be made by the teacher to guide the acquisition of these sounds, as the order of acquisition is random and cannot be controlled.

- At some point in the future, students will be able to hear and say all of the sounds of English.

New View

Not surprisingly, the New View of how English learners come to master the phonology of English is a bit different. Like any other system, the sound system of a language can be analyzed, categorized, labeled, taught, and measured. Because there is a "right" or "locally correct" way of using sounds, there must be a plan in place to ensure that students indeed master them as soon as possible. Here are the key points:

- The number of sounds in English can be determined; there is general agreement that they sum to 44.

- These sounds can be taught in order, beginning with those that are easiest to produce.

- The ear must be taught not only to hear sounds, but also to be able to distinguish between subtle differences in tone, emphasis, and rhythm.

- Producing English sounds correctly is largely a related set of physical activities: moving the mouth, tongue, jaw, and face muscles, while simultaneously controlling the force, volume, velocity, and movement of air from the lungs (sometimes diaphragm) and out through the mouth (and sometimes nose).

- Hearing the sounds and making the sounds is normative: one either hears or says them correctly, or not. Thus, mastery is the goal.

- Students learning to hear and produce the sounds of English will need direct instruction, feedback, and overt correction to master them as soon as possible.

- If allowed, students new to English will make errors that to them sound "right," frequently leading to *Pidgin* versions of the language. If their peers make the same errors, they will all agree that they are speaking English "correctedly." Get it?

As we will see, the classroom methods that correlate to each view are quite different. In the Old View, teachers would just be asked to talk, and to perhaps slow down their rate of speech, repeat key words, and encourage students to say new words. In the New View, teachers take a proactive approach to developing both the receptive and productive elements of English. Let's learn what those are and how they not only can help students to learn to speak correctly, but also can accelerate development of their phonological skills.

Reading Comprehension Connection

Unfortunately, most teachers have had the experience of listening to English learners read aloud in English in ways that display their full inventory of phonology problems and underdeveloped sound system. In the primary grades, reading teachers help students to crack the code of letter-sound relationships. By fourth grade, students are reading and learning about concepts and ideas that frequently bring with them multi-syllabic words that are used nowhere else. What these classroom scenarios have in common is their reliance on students' possessing full mastery of English phonology. If a student pronounces all words that start with the letter y as /j/, and all *th* clusters as /d/, we end up with:

Do ju know dat da settlers arrived in California many jears in da past?

Similarly, how can English learners in primary grades be expected to count the phonemes in the word "cat" if their ear cannot hear those sounds? How can spelling be taught to a student who is still not producing the sounds correctly? Finally, for students in upper grades who are bombarded with new vocabulary words all day long from the mouths of fast-talking teachers, how are they to hear and be able to say words like *constitutional, multiplication,* and *deoxyribonucleic acid*? From these examples we can see that phonology for English learners has much more to do with reading comprehension than we may have thought at first glance.

 ## Academic Writing Connection

Do your best to read with comprehension this sentence produced by an intermediate-level English learner in eighth grade.

Iz Imporand to haf naluj to solva prombles in maths and use coreck formula.

Collect a hundred essays from English learners at most any grade level and really look at the spelling errors. You will quickly see patterns that show students' poor phonology control impacts in a very negative way their ability to spell. Once older students recognize that their ear cannot be trusted to figure out spellings, isn't it logical that they would retreat to the comfort of the same inventory of words that they know how to spell and that they have been using for years in essays of all persuasions? If we want students to spell words correctly based on fairly predictable letter-sound relationships, we need to ensure that they can hear and say the sounds first.

> ***Students need*** *the ability to correctly hear and produce the sounds of the English language clearly.*

Language Warm-up

Description

Through guided instruction and practice, students learn to both aurally distinguish and then orally produce the unique sounds of the English language. This method employs 10 specific listening and speaking drills that can be used and combined in a variety of ways to target students' specific oral language needs and deficits.

Purpose

One of the first means by which native and second-language speakers of a language are identified is through their mastery of the sounds of a language. Training students to both hear and say the sounds of English not only enables basic communication, but also assists with phonetically decoding text and spelling the words of the English language. In simple language, the purpose of the drills in this method is to develop native-like English oral fluency and tune the ear to have native-like receptive competence.

Materials Needed

- ☐ English language alphabet chart
- ☐ Numbers chart (1-100)
- ☐ Student journals and/or worksheets
- ☐ Chart paper

Teacher Skills

- ✓ knowledge of the 44 phonemes of the English language and their articulation
- ✓ knowledge of current student independent language level
- ✓ awareness of language level that students should be pushed to during the lesson
- ✓ ability to form and manage students in pairs/groups to share answers
- ✓ ability to listen for and correct pronunciation errors
- ✓ ability to move through sequenced drills quickly while insisting on accuracy

Language Objective: We will hear, produce, and tell the difference between sounds in English.

Steps

This method is a collection of 10 drills, or exercises, that are done almost entirely orally. The goal here is oral accuracy, meaning the teacher must be prepared to conduct a quick-paced lesson in which students must constantly produce and listen attentively.

Language Warm-up can last anywhere from five to 60 minutes. All 10 exercises can be practiced in one day or the lesson can extend over the course of a week through various combinations of activities. Whether practicing one of the 10 exercises or all, each *Language Warm-up* lesson should be guided by a focus on a particular sound in the English language based on student need.

In planning the lesson, two things must first be decided:

☐ What sound(s) will be the language focus of the lesson?
☐ Which activities will be used to practice this focus?

To assist you in determining the language focus of the lesson, refer to the table of English phonemes on the following pages. Lessons can focus on one sound, multiple sounds, or multiple spellings of one sound.

	PHONEME	GRAPHEME	EXAMPLES
1	/b/	b, bb	big, rubber
2	/d/	d, dd, ed	dog, add, filled
3	/f/	f, ph	fish, phone
4	/g/	g, gg	go, egg
5	/h/	h	hot
6	/j/	j, g, ge, dge	jet, cage, barge, judge
7	/k/	c, k, ck, ch, cc, que	cat, kitten, duck, school, occur, antique
8	/l/	l, ll	leg, bell
9	/m/	m, mm, mb	mad, hammer, lamb
10	/n/	n, nn, kn, gn	no, dinner, knee, gnome
11	/p/	p, pp	pie, apple
12	/r/	r, rr, wr	run, marry, write
13	/s/	s, se, ss, c, ce, sc	sun, mouse, dress, city, ice, science
14	/t/	t, tt, ed	top, letter, stopped
15	/v/	v, ve	vet, give
16	/w/	w	wet, win, swim
17	/y/	y, i	yes, onion
18	/z/	z, zz, ze, s, se, x	zip, fizz, sneeze, laser, is, xylophone
19	short /a/	a, au	hat, laugh
20	short /e/	e, ea	bed, bread
21	short /i/	i	if
22	short /o/	o, a, au, aw, ough	hot, want, haul, draw, bought
23	short /u/	u, o	up, ton
24	long /a/	a, a_e, ay, ai, ey, ei	bacon, late, day, train, they, vein
25	long /e/	e, e_e, ea, ee, ey, ie, y	me, these, beat, feet, key, chief, baby

	PHONEME	GRAPHEME	EXAMPLES
26	long /i/	i, i_e, igh, y, ie	find, ride, light, fly, pie
27	long /o/	o, o_e, oa, ou, ow	no, note, boat, sould, row
28	long /u/	u, u_e, ew	human, use, few, chew
29	/th/ - not voiced	th	thumb, thin, thing
30	/th/ - voiced	th	this, feather, then
31	/ng/	ng, n	sing, monkey, sink
32	/sh/	sh, ss, ch, ti, ci	ship, mission, chef, motion, special
33	/ch/	ch, tch	chip, match
34	/zh/	ge, s	garage, measure, division
35	/wh/ - with breath	wh	what, when, where, why
36	/oo/	oo, u, oul	book, put, could
37	/oo/	oo, u, u_e	moon, truth, rule
38	/ow/	ow, ou, ou_e	cow, out, mouse, house
39	/oy/	oi, oy	coin, toy
40	/a(r)/	ar	car
41	/a(r)/	air, ear, are	air, chair, fair, hair, bear, care
42	/i(r)/	irr, ere, eer	mirror, here, cheer
43	/o(r)/	or, ore, oor	for, core, door
44	/u(r)/	ur, ir, er, ear, or, ar	burn, first, fern, heard, work, dollar

Once a target sound or sounds have been selected, decide which of the following activities will be used to practice pronunciation and sound distinction. The *Language Warm-up* method consists of 10 independently instructed activities that together form a complete phonology teaching sequence. As mentioned previously, the methods can be taught during one lesson or over the course of a week.

Within each activity, there are many ways to instruct the focus sound. Because this method relies on consistent oral practice, teachers should utilize a variety of instructional strategies to keep the method fresh and exciting. We will discuss the description, possible instruction, and preparation for each of the following activities individually.

Activities

1. Alphabet Recognition and Letter Sound Practice
2. Numbers Practice
3. Minimal Pairs/Phrases/Sentences
4. Repeat After Me
5. Count the Words
6. Rhythm Exercise
7. Intonation
8. Tongue Twister
9. Dictation
10. Antonyms/Synonyms

1. Alphabet Recognition and Sound Practice

Students identify letters by name and pronounce letter sounds or identify letters based on sound.

Possible Instruction:

- Students say alphabet out loud, in order.
- Students say alphabet out loud, backwards.
- Teacher points to one specific letter, students say aloud.
- Students read a line of letters, out of order.
- Students say all vowels.
- Students say all consonants.
- Students are asked to spell their names, names of others.
- Students are asked to say the name of the fifth letter, third letter, second letter, etc.
- Students are asked to spell classroom items. "What are the letters in the word, _____?"
- Teacher points to a letter. Students make the sound.
- "What sound does the sixth letter make?" Twelfth letter, twentieth letter, etc.
- Teacher whispers or silently mouths a sound. Students identify the letter.

- _____

(Write your own!)

Preparation/Materials Needed

- ☐ alphabet chart
- ☐ focus phoneme
- ☐ lesson plan

2. Numbers Practice

Students accurately say and identify numbers.

Possible Instruction:

- Students count forward from chart, from 0-50, 1-100, etc.
- Students count backward from 50, 40, 10, etc.
- Students count by 2s, 3s, 5s, 10s, etc.
- Teacher points to a number and students say it aloud.
- Teacher whispers or silently mouths a number. Students identify the number.
- Teacher says a number and students identify the individual digits in the number.
- Teacher gives the digits of the number and students identify the number.
- Students read an equation using the academic terms ("The sum of six and two is eight.")

- _____
(Write your own!)

Preparation/Materials Needed

- ☐ number chart
- ☐ focus phoneme
- ☐ lesson plan

Tip!

Even though the above activity is called number practice, the purpose of the method is still to practice saying and hearing sounds. Select your target sound *first* and then think about which numbers will require students to produce that sound. For example, if your focus is /f/, try numbers like forty, fifty, fifteen, three fifths, etc.

3. Minimal Pairs/Phrases/Sentences

Students aurally distinguish between two words, phrases, or sentences

Possible Instruction:

- Teacher says two words. Students indicate with a hand signal or in writing if the words sound the <u>same</u> or <u>different.</u>
- Teacher says two phrases. Students indicate with a hand signal or in writing if the phrases are the <u>same</u> or <u>different.</u>
- Teacher says two sentences. Students indicate with a hand signal or in writing if the sentences are the <u>same</u> or <u>different</u>.

- _____

(Write your own!)

Preparation/Materials Needed

- ☐ list of minimal pairs
- ☐ focus phoneme
- ☐ lesson plan

Minimal Pairs Samples

1.	fin thin		21.	sip zip		41.	bliss blouse
2.	fret threat		22.	close clothes		42.	blind blur
3.	Fred thread		23.	dice dies		43.	bleed blade
4.	oaf oath		24.	sewn zone		44.	claim flame
5.	deaf death		25.	fuss fuzz		45.	clear clinic
6.	lay ray		26.	shrill thrill		46.	clef club
7.	low row		27.	shank thank		47.	flask glass
8.	lake rake		28.	harsh heart		48.	flew glue
9.	goal gore		29.	rash rath		49.	fled glade
10.	lung rung		30.	tin thin		50.	float flight
11.	seat sheet		31.	true threw		51.	flood flock
12.	sealed shield		32.	tank thank		52.	glow plow
13.	sake shake		33.	tong thong		53.	glitter gloom
14.	sore shore		34.	tug thug		54.	place slice
15.	sail shale		35.	teeth teethe		55.	please sleeve
16.	sigh thigh		36.	ether either		56.	plight slight
17.	sank thank		37.	thee Z		57.	plant pledge
18.	sink think		38.	breathe breeze		58.	plant plod
19.	sump thump		39.	blast class		59.	sled splurge
20.	mass math		40.	blue clue		60.	slope pop

MINIMAL PHRASES

1. to the door / to the store
2. out at night / out of sight
3. now's the time / now it's mine
4. once upon a time / once upon a mime
5. over and out / over and out
6. six silly snakes / six silly snacks
7. raining cats and dogs / raining cats and hogs
8. little yellow kitty / little yellow mitty
9. green grass everywhere / green grass over there
10. for the night / for the right
11. a new microscope/a new microscope
12. planets orbiting the sun/planets are orbiting the sun
13. the stomach scrunches/the stomach crunches
14. conjugating variable verbs/conjugating variant verbs
15. subject pronouns are easy/subset pronouns are easy
16. eight parts of speech/eight parts of speech
17. nineteen hundred thirty three/nine hundred and thirty three
18. 55.5 times .5/55.55 times .5
19. exciting summer ELD fun/exciting summer ED fun
20. proper pronunciation with practice/practice with proper pronunciation

MINIMAL SENTENCES

1. It's good to be home. / It's good to be in Rome.
2. I saw the man cleaning. / I saw the man leaning.
3. Run as fast as you can to the store. / Run faster than you can to the store.
4. Turn the light out in the hall. / Turn the white out in the fall.
5. I walked and talked all night long. / I walk and talk all night long.
6. How can you say that to me at this time? / How can you say it's mine at this time?
7. Don't run on the blacktop or you'll fall. / Don't run on the blacktop in the fall.
8. Math is a subject full of facts. / Math is a suitcase full of acts.
9. Pass me the tissue, if you please. / Pass me the tissue or I'll sneeze.
10. The leaves on the ground turned red and greed. / The leaves all around turned red and green.
11. Math vocabulary can be tricky at times. / Math vocabulary can be sticky at times.
12. A city certainly needs people to do different jobs. / A city certainly needs people to choose different jobs.
13. Nouns and verbs are very exciting to me. / Nouns and verbs are very exciting to me.
14. A better summer I have never had! / A better summer I had never had!
15. Adding the numbers 33 and 13 gives you 46. / Adding the numbers 30.3 and 13 gives you 43.6.

4. Repeat After Me

Students completely and accurately repeat a sentence said by the teacher.

Possible Instruction:

- Teacher says a complete sentence (no chunking) once and students chorally repeat the sentence exactly with correct pronunciation, intonation, and rhythm.
- Teacher says a complete sentence once and students produce the sentence word-by-word, student-by-student.
- Teacher says a complete sentence and students identify the fourth word, last word, tenth word, etc.
- After correctly repeating the sentence, students say the sentence backwards.
- _____

(Write your own!)

Preparation/Materials Needed

☐ prepared sentence
☐ focus phoneme
☐ lesson plan

5. Count the Words

Students count the words in a sentence said by the teacher.

Possible Instruction:

- Teacher says a complete sentence (no chunking) once and students verbally give the number of words in the sentence.
- Teacher says a complete sentence once and students write down the number of words in the sentence (on paper or white boards).
- _____

(Write your own!)

Preparation/Materials Needed

☐ prepared sentence
☐ focus phoneme
☐ lesson plan

Tip!

- Have students count the words in a sentence before using the "Repeat After Me" exercise.
- Students will want to count the words on their fingers as the sentence is being read. Instead, ask students to try to see the entire sentence in their heads as it's being read. Only allow students to count on their fingers AFTER the completion of the sentence.

SAMPLE SENTENCES FOR REPEAT AFTER ME/ COUNT THE WORDS

Science

1. Scientists would learn about life from the past if they studied fossils hidden in the Earth.

2. While in space, the astronaut should observe the Earth's moon by charting its movement and patterns.

3. Long ago, scientists knew that California's landscapes would change due to fires and floods.

4. What would you use to show a solid changing into a liquid?

5. The explosions on Mars's surface must be changing that planet's exterior.

6. If you wanted to reduce the heat in your car, you could tint your windows to block out the sun's rays.

7. As long as frogs lay their eggs in a safe place, the life cycle should continue.

8. Freezing and thawing temperatures would cause rocks to break down into smaller pieces.

9. All matter is made up of atoms, which may combine to form molecules.

10. Scientists should make predications based on their observations and not their opinions.

Math

1. The math student is correctly plotting the coordinates on the graph during his test.

2. Multiplying two numbers together will be challenging for students in _____ (insert grade) grade.

3. The teacher explains the answer while she writes the mathematical steps on the board.

4. The ambitious students are adding up their scores as the teacher is returning their tests.

5. Several _____ (insert grade) graders accurately describe the formation of a right angle to their partner before drawing it on their paper.

6. Our math book provides several examples of how to solve complicated equations.

Social Science

1. Transportation has changed dramatically over the last 100 years.

2. Every community has included important public services by adding police and fire departments.

3. The President of the United States has generated some important ideas on how to save our country money.

4. Citizens have participated in the democratic process by voting for political candidates.

5. Communities have grown over time due to the increased construction of houses, gas stations, and restaurants.

6. Local strawberry farmers have sold their fruit to community grocery stores for consumers to purchase.

7. Elementary school students wrote letters to the mayor thanking him for his visit last week.

8. My family has traveled to the mountains, seen the desert, spent three days in the rainforest, and walked near a swamp.

9. For our last field trip, the bus driver consulted different maps in order to find the location of our destination.

10. Over the last six months, various community members have assisted in our classroom by reading stories and explaining math problems.

ELA

1. The main character of the story changed from the beginning of the novel to the end.

2. Plot, setting, and character are all literary elements.

3. Combining sentences forms a paragraph and combining paragraphs forms an essay.

4. Different punctuation marks change the tone of sentences.

5. Before writing the essay, the student should have outlined the main idea and details.

6. Quotation marks should be used to include dialogue in text.

7. The major genres of literature are drama, tragedy, comedy, romance, and satire.

8. Don't forget to leave an indent when starting a new paragraph.

9. If the setting had been different, the climax of the story would not have been possible.

10. Many poems include various types of rhyme throughout the stanzas.

6. Rhythm Exercise

Students orally produce a string of letters, numbers, etc. following the same beat demonstrated by the teacher.

Possible Instruction:

- Teacher demonstrates rhythm and students mimic:
    - <u>a</u>-<u>b</u>-<u>c</u>-<u>d</u>
    - <u>a</u> and <u>b</u> and <u>c</u> and <u>d</u>
    - <u>a</u> and then a <u>b</u> and then a <u>c</u> and then a <u>d</u>
    - <u>a</u> and then put a <u>b</u> and then put a <u>c</u> and then put a <u>d</u>
- Students practice in pairs and then demonstrate for class as class claps along.

- _____

(Write your own!)

Preparation/Materials Needed

- ☐ prepared rhythm
- ☐ focus phoneme
- ☐ lesson plan

> **Tip!**
>
> - Have students read the rhythm before adding the beat.
> - Ask students to clap along to practice the beat.
> - The underlined letters in the examples can be replaced with any letters, numbers, or words that align with your language objective (example: <u>b</u> and <u>v</u> and <u>v</u> and <u>b</u>).

7. Intonation

Students repeat a phrase or sentence practicing different intonation.

Possible Instruction:

- Teacher shows a sentence for students to read with different emotion (surprise, boredom, confusion, etc.) *You arrived on time.*
- Teacher shows a sentence for students to read with different intonation based on punctuation (declarative, interrogative, imperative, exclamatory). *My dog is lost.*

- _____

(Write your own!)

Preparation/Materials Needed

- ☐ prepared sentence/phrase
- ☐ focus phoneme
- ☐ lesson plan

8. Tongue Twister

Students repeat a tongue twister to increase language fluency.

Possible Instruction:

- Teacher reads a tongue twister. Students practice reading the words and then practice reciting the tongue twister with fluency.
- Students practice a tongue twister in pairs or as homework and recite in front of the class.
- _____

(Write your own!)

Preparation/Materials Needed

- ☐ prepared tongue twister
- ☐ focus phoneme
- ☐ lesson plan

Tongue Twisters

A

My dame hath a lame tame crane,
My dame hath a crane that is lame.

B

A box of biscuits, a batch of mixed biscuits

Brad's big black bath brush broke.

A big black bug bit a big black bear,
made the big black bear bleed blood.

C

Crisp crusts crackle crunchily.

Copper coffee cup

D

Does the doctor diagnose other doctors?

E

Ed had edited it.

F

I have felt a lot of felt.

Fred fed Ted bread, and Ted fed Fred bread

Friendly Frank flips fine flapjacks.

Fat frogs flying past fast.

Flee from fog to fight flu fast!

G

Gertie's great-grandma grew aghast at Gertie's grammar.

Greek grapes

Three gray geese in the green grass grazing. Gray were the geese and green was the grass.

Girl gargoyle, guy gargoyle

I

Inchworms itching.

K

Unique New York.

Kris Kringle carefully crunched on candy canes.

L

Lovely lemon and limes

M

The myth of Miss Muffet

Mix, Miss Mix!

Can you imagine an imaginary menagerie manager?

N

A noisy noise annoys an oyster.

Many an anemone sees an enemy anemone.

Nine nice night nurse nursing nicely.

O

Old oily autos

P

Peter Piper picked a peck of pickled peppers.

R

Truly rural

S

A skunk sat on a stump and stunk.

Six thick thistle sticks.

I slit the sheet, and on the sheet I sit.

She sells sea shells by the sea shore.

Mrs. Smith's Fish Sauce Shop.

Sam's shop stocks short spotted socks.

Moose noshing much mush.

T

Toy boat

Tim is the thin twin.

The two-twenty-two train tore through the tunnel.

Twelve twins twirled twelve twigs.

V

Vincent vowed vengeance very vehemently.

W

Which wristwatches are Swiss wristwatches?

Which witch wished which wicked wish?

9. Dictation

Students write down letters, numbers, words, phrases, or sentences exactly as the teacher dictates them.

Possible Instruction:

- *License Plate* game. The teacher says a series of from three to 10 of the units listed below. Students write down exactly what they hear.
    - letters
    - numbers
    - punctuation marks
    - sounds
    - words
- Teacher says an entire sentence and students copy it down.

- For example: 2unx153, or, $35.76XT5U6

- _____

_____

(Write your own!)

Preparation/Materials Needed

- ☐ prepared dictation
- ☐ focus phoneme
- ☐ lesson plan

10. Antonyms/Synonyms

Students practice words of similar and opposite meaning.

Possible Instruction:

- Teacher introduces a word and teaches a synonym or antonym for the word using one of the following frames:

antonyms

- ○ _____ is an antonym for _____.
- ○ _____ is the opposite of _____.
- ○ _____ is the inverse of _____.

synonyms

- ○ _____ is a synonym for _____.
- ○ _____ means the same as _____.
- ○ _____ is similar to _____.

- Teacher uses the above frames but has students spell the words.
- Using the above frames, students name as many antonyms/synonyms as they can within a given time period.

- _____
_____
(Write your own!)

Preparation/Materials Needed

- ☐ prepared antonyms/synonyms
- ☐ focus phoneme
- ☐ lesson plan

Tip!

Keep a running list of synonyms and antonyms as the class progresses.

Discussion of Steps

Before the lesson begins

Create the Lesson Plan

- Select the focus sound(s) based on student need.
- Decide how many activities students will complete/day.
  - The lesson plan template that follows can be used to guide weekly lessons. It is designed for daily lessons of 20-60 minutes.
  - An example of a 30-minute/day weekly plan has also been provided.
- Assure that students will have paper or whiteboards available any written response exercises.

Lesson Plan Template

Week_____   Focus: _____

	Monday	Tuesday	Wednesday	Thursday	Friday
Alphabet Letters and Sounds (5 min.)					
Numbers (5 min.)					
Minimal Pairs (3 min.)					
Count the Words (2 min.)					*Quiz*
Repeat After Me (5 min.)					
Antonyms/ Synonyms (5 min.)					
Other					

Sample Weekly Plan
Week 9/3   Focus: /b/ /v/

	Monday	Tuesday	Wednesday	Thursday	
Alphabet Letters and Sounds (5 min.)	-alphabet backwards -all consonants - b v g e c t (letters, sounds) -mouth sounds	-all vowels - d p v b (letters, then sounds) -spell synonyms from yesterday	-every other letter a-z (girls, then boys) -what sound: --2nd letter? --22nd? 4th?	-Say sounds, students identify: -d, v, b, g, t, e, c, p -Students whisper sounds and other students identify letter	
Numbers (5 min.)	-74, 45, 75, 500 (numbers and digits) -count by 5s from 0-50	-count by 5s from 50-0 -78 173 572 15.07 (give digits, students identify #)	-count by 5s from 50-100 -79 107 712 577 (give number)	-count by 5s from 100-50 79-12=67 500/100=5	
Minimal Pairs (3 min.)	bat-vat, bet-vet, bit-bit vase-vase, base-base, bee-vee, vile-vile We bow. - We vow.	love-lub, live-lib, rove-robe, give-give, gave-gabe, Are the vans ready? Are the vans ready?	over-over, lubber-lover, gibbon-given, dribble-drivel, loaves-lobes, This is the best! This is the vest!	boat-vote, berry-very, curb-curve, verb-verve, fiber- fiver, The beeper vibrates. The beeper vibrates.	
Count the Words (2 min.)	The river otters bask in the sun every day before breakfast. (11)	Some mammals hibernate every winter because of the cold. (9)	In the evening, birds often gather together by crowding into the same tree. (13)	Ferociously, the starving bobcat bared its teeth to the very frightened squirrel. (12)	**Friday Quiz**
Repeat After Me (5 min.)	The river otters bask in the sun every day before breakfast.	Some mammals hibernate every winter because of the cold.	In the evening, birds often gather together by crowding into the same tree.	Ferociously, the starving bobcat bared its teeth to the very frightened squirrel	
Antonyms/ Synonyms (5 min.)	synonyms: bother-annoy before-prior vicious-ferocious	synonyms: evening-dusk donate-give discover-find	antonyms: before-after vicious-docile evening-morning	antonyms: give-accept find-lose annoy-charm	
Other	**Rhythm/Intonation/Dictation/Tongue Twister**				
	Rhythm: -b v v b -b and v and v and b -b and then a v and then a v and then a b	Intonation: My best friend is very beautiful. (declarative, interrogative, exclamatory)	Dictation: b d e p v /v/ /b/ 575 17 The boys have very nice voices.	Tongue Twister: Betty loves the velvet vest best.	

During the Lesson

Follow the activity description and steps for each of the activities you will be using throughout the *Language Warm-up* lesson. Here are some general tips to remember during the lesson.

- Maintain a quick pace. Students respond immediately through oral production or gestures. Each activity should last no more than a few minutes with the focus on as much *accurate* student production as possible.
- Create an environment that mimics a conversational setting. Instead of arranging the desks in standard rows where students look only at the teacher and the backs of other students' heads, try forming a circle or a "u." Some activities can be done with students standing and facing each other. Students must be able to distinguish the sounds from other students, not just the teacher.
- Enforce accuracy. This method targets the sounds of English. Now is the time to correct mispronunciations while training for rhythm and intonation. Do students *sound* as much like native speakers as possible?
- Challenge students. If the activities within the method remain the same, it is likely that both the students and the teacher will tire of them. Try the listed variations within each activity. The lesson should present a challenge in the focus sound and/or the activities used.

Assessment

Student proficiency with the sounds of the English language can be assessed in many ways. Below are a few examples.

- ✓ Have students keep weekly journals of their *Language Warm-up* activities. Grade them weekly.
- ✓ As shown on the provided lesson plan template, one day/week (or every other week) can be used as an assessment day. Proceed through each of the activities listed, but have students write down their responses rather than saying them.
- ✓ Ask students to practice an oral presentation weekly or biweekly. An oral presentation utilizes many of the language skills students have been practicing throughout the week. Examples for presentation topics and a scoring rubric are provided below.

Suggestions for Oral Presentations

Beginners	Intermediate	Advanced
School Pledge/Chant	Pledge of Allegiance	Star-Spangled Banner
Nursery Rhyme	What you will do after school?	*The Night Before Christmas*
What did you eat for dinner?	*This or That* (three sentences)	What are your plans for the coming weekend?
This or That (1 sentence)	*Function Junction* (three sentences)	*This or That* (five sentences)
Function Junction (one sentence)	Tongue twister stories	*Function Junction* (five sentences)
Tongue twisters	Simple poems	What verb tense are you learning about and why?
	School rules/Class rules	Preamble to the Constitution
Name all of the parts of speech in a complete sentence.		
How do you get home from school?	Use all of the parts of speech in a complete sentence correctly.	Explain the function of each part of speech using complete sentences.
What kinds of animals live in_____ (particular habitat).	Name the continents and describe their location.	Explain of the life cycle of _____.
Name all of the continents.	Name all of the planets and describe their distance from the Earth or the sun.	Name all of the continents and oceans and describe their location.
Where and when you were born	Your favorite activity when you were younger	What you were like when you were small child
Name some of the people that work in the community.	Describe one community job.	What will you do when you graduate from high school?
What classes are you taking this semester?	What classes will you take next semester?	How can you exit the ELD program?

Oral Presentation Scoring Guide

Presentation Length

Beginner = 30 seconds
Intermediate = 45 seconds
Advanced = 60 seconds

Scoring Guide

- No errors= 6 points
- 1-2 errors= 5 points
- 3-4 errors= 4 points
- 5-6 errors= 3 points
- 7-8 errors = 2 points
- > 9 errors= 0 points

Phonology	_____ / 6
Morphology	_____ / 6
Syntax	_____ / 6
Vocabulary	_____ / 6
Proper Time	_____ / 6
Total Score	_____ /30

How to count errors

*It is easiest to count errors if the teacher has a written copy of what the student will present.

1. *Phonology- pronunciation*
   For every phonological error/mispronunciation, count one error. For example, if the student tries to say "they" but pronounces "day."

2. *Morphology- word endings, sub./verb agreement*
   Count one error for every suffix or prefix that the student misses or misuses and for every incorrect verb conjugation. For example, "We going to the store."

3. *Vocabulary- using correct word in context*
   Count one error for words that are used in inappropriate context. For example, "We *built* a cake." (Instead of we *made/baked* a cake.)

4. *Syntax- use of complete sentences/variety*
   Count one error for every incomplete sentence. Subtract one point *on the third time* a structure is repeated. For example using "I like" in every sentence.

5. *Proper time*
   Count one error for every second short of the time goal. Example: Beginner presentation = 25 seconds= 5 errors = -3 points.

Tip: At the beginning, it may be helpful to have more than one teacher do the scoring so that differences can be discussed and a more calibrated system developed.

What the *Language Warm-up* looks like across the language levels

Language Warm-up can be practiced with any language level though the activities and focus may change. The method is very useful for beginner students as they are introduced to the sounds of the English language. Intermediate students, on the other hand, should practice challenging phoneme distinctions and blends, such as /b/ versus /v/ and /th/ versus /d/. Finally, as students continue to strive toward sounding as much like native speakers as possible, they can work on intonation, rhythm, and multisyllabic words and should also practice academic vocabulary within the method.

While the activities used remain the same for all language levels, the content should differ. Here are some examples for each of the ten exercises discussed.

Activity	Beginner	Intermediate	Advanced
Alphabet Recognition/ Letter Sounds	letters and sounds in isolation	blends, letters out of order, short words	multisyllabic words
Numbers	1-100	1-1,000, short equations	academic math terms (fractions, decimals, etc.)
Minimal Pairs/Phrases	letters, sounds, single syllable words	sounds, words, phrases	multisyllabic words, phrases, sentences, equations
Count the Words	10 words or less	10-20 words	20 words or more
Repeat After Me	10 words or less	10-20 words	20 words or more
Rhythm	letters, sounds and single-syllable numbers in isolation	letters, sounds, short words, phrases, longer numbers	sounds, words, phrases, math terms
Intonation	one word or short phrase	short phrase or sentence	phrases, sentences, academic content
Tongue Twister	five words or less	five-10 words	10 words or more
Dictation	letters, sounds, numbers 1-100, punctuation	blends, short words, phrases, numbers 1-1,000, sentences	phrases, multisyllabic words, academic math terms, sentences
Antonyms/Synonyms	basic vocabulary (hot/cold, smart/intelligent, etc.)	basic and academic words (hot/scorching)	academic content (transformation/ metamorphosis)

What this Method *Isn't*

It's not the time for the teacher to practice his/her language. The method done correctly should involve students producing *more* than the teacher.

It's not choral reading or reciting. To accurately assess each student's language ability, students must be given the opportunity to produce individually and receive feedback.

It's not chanting the alphabet repeatedly. Many of us have learned to "sing along" to the alphabet song or count from 1-10 in another language. Provide students with the opportunity to practice letters and numbers out of order to assure that they can produce both the names and the sounds when not simply singing along.

It's not a read along with the teacher. To keep students from simply mimicking either you or other students, turn off the teacher voice when it's time for a student to produce and ask other students to do the same.

Things to Re-think

From these methods and the discussion at the beginning of this chapter contrasting views of how students learn phonology, we can see that the New View takes a very proactive approach. As you reviewed and perhaps tried some of these methods, spend a moment re-thinking a few things.

Administrators' Corner

What to look for in *Language Warm-up*

➜ Is the method clearly labeled?

➜ Are the resources in place? An alphabet chart? Number chart? Prepared lesson plan?

➜ Are students situated to allow for maximum sound production practice?

➜ Are student errors immediately corrected?

➜ Is there a clear sound focus for the lesson?

➜ Are the activities within the method brief, lasting only a few minutes each?

➜ Do students have the opportunity to listen and respond to each other?

➜ Does the teacher read along with the students or allow students to produce on their own?

➜ Do different language level classrooms show different levels of student production?

1. To which view can we attribute the troubling trend among English learners in upper grades who, after years in school sitting in English-speaking classrooms, still struggle with English pronunciation and hearing words clearly?

2. Which view of language holds the most promise for providing English learners with a solid start and foundation in phonology?

3. What educational, social and economic implications are there for English learners who never truly master phonology?

4. What do Mel Gibson, Antonio Banderas and Gwyneth Paltrow all have in common? (Answer: They all regularly employ phonology coaches to help them master new accents.)

5. Was Henry Higgins unreasonable in his quest for perfect pronunciation from Eliza? Were his methods those of a crazy linguist or those of a linguistic pragmatist and teacher?

What to Expect

If you are trying these methods for the first time with English learners who have never been "taught" proper pronunciation, here are a few things you both can probably expect:

➢ Your pace will initially be slow as you work through the method. It may feel mechanical at first, and not possess the flow you probably desire.

➢ Be prepared for students to look at you like dogs hearing a siren. What in the world is going on here, they will ask with quizzical faces. "Are you kidding me?" is a likely reaction from older students. Remember, they have faked their way through this for years, laughing their way on to the next pronunciation blunder or avoidance technique. By way of analogy, they are out of shape when it comes to using their muscles and air to form sounds that mimic native speakers.

➢ Your administrator and perhaps even colleagues will think you have taken a left turn. After all, they too were told not to worry about pronunciation, that it comes naturally. Be prepared to explain in detail the rationale for doing this.

➢ In its most brutal form, others may think you are seeking to embarrass, harass or call out students with these drills. What a strange reaction to helping students with something that is the most obvious manifestation of their English proficiency.

➢ After two weeks of doing these drills consistently, you will have developed an incredible group of supporters for teaching phonology: your students. They have always known of their phonology challenges and have now finally found someone who will help them. Good work.

Voices from the Classroom

Language Warm Up has greatly increased my awareness of the nuances of the English language. I teach middle school age students who are mostly beginning English learners. Using the Language Warm Up method provides me with an opportunity to teach the subtleties of the language that are inherent in native speakers and to correct the habits that my students pick up when socializing with native speakers or more advanced language learners. It allows for more instances of conversation about what is "natural" and what will sound "normal" to the general population. My students have been able to realize that emphasis and accents placed on words or phrases can change the meaning for their intended audience.

I have found it interesting to teach and a challenge to my own language skills when having to focus on particular pronunciations of words or phrases. As a native speaker, I, too, have picked up "bad habits" that amount to the development of an "accent" when I speak. I have had to correct these in myself at times, while providing an explanation of why or how it happens to my students. Planning lessons for my beginning students has given me more opportunities to introduce more casually and commonly used vocabulary, which I find invaluable because, in most cases, my classroom is the only place where they are required to practice their English, so hearing and pronouncing words, phrases, and sentences correctly helps them feel confident enough to use their skills elsewhere.– Kristin from Newark, CA

Language Warm-up forces the students to listen carefully to proper English. A challenge is that they wanted me to repeat everything at first. However, by not repeating myself, they have learned to pay attention. My advice is to practice the steps in Language Warm-up and to have signals for procedures in the method so that it goes as smoothly as possible from the start. I also recommend having a designated spot in your classroom where the letters, numbers, and synonyms/antonyms can remain through the year.

*A success I have had with Language warm-up is that my students are starting to say synonyms or antonyms of words we are using in class, even when it isn't Language Warm-up time. My students are confident and are motivated to express the language they have learned.-*Carrie from Yuma, AZ

Language Functions

Old View

As we have seen in previous chapters, a pure rendering of the Old View comes across as adherence to rules, regulations, and requirements. Many remember from high school or college such approaches that were heavy on the knowing of language forms but light on the application. It is valid criticism to suggest that the Old View, particularly in its Classical incarnation, placed little emphasis on the use of the language in what could be called regular communicative contexts, e.g., talking with a friend, ordering food, or crafting an essay for a class assignment. But we must remember that many of the precepts associated with the Old View came from times long ago, when languages were taught and learned for reasons quite different from the interactive contexts listed above. Instead, language was frequently taught and learned in order to translate materials, or to study ancient texts. Such tasks required an impeccable grasp of grammar rules in two or more languages, since frequently the goal was literal rendering of a text or document from one language to another, or the careful parsing of a particular word, sentence, or passage.

A second reason for the early appeal of grammar-heavy approaches was that they were consistent with learning theory at the time. The Newtonian revolution and subsequent developments in thinking, particularly from the sciences, endorsed a mechanistic paradigm wherein big things were micro-analyzed into their smallest components. By studying those smaller components, one could gain a better understanding of the big thing. Language lent itself to such an analysis beautifully; it could be distilled into small units, and then reassembled.

Of course, the problem was that putting the little pieces back together into something that had meaning was not always emphasized. Plus, it was hard to do. Faced with an inventory of little components and a desire to perform a big linguistic task (for example, to ask what might have happened if event *y* were to have occurred and not event *x*), many language learners quickly figured out that simple language tasks were easier. *¿Cómo estás?* is certainly simpler than inquiring (in Spanish) as to whether one would feel better if the weather were perhaps different.

This analytic, part-to-whole approach produced in many cases students who knew *about* language but could not *do* language.

Critics of the classical paradigm and its methods went a very different direction beginning in the 1970s by essentially eschewing it all in favor of a different set of beliefs, what we call Old View 2.0. These beliefs, as we have seen earlier, called for the abolition of grammar teaching, an emphasis on communication and authenticity and a guiding axiom that language was acquired, not learned. Whether intended or not, educators heard that language did not need to be taught as a subject area. Students would just get it through osmosis as a function of time spent hearing English.

New View

As you will see with the *Function Junction* method coming up in this chapter, our New View hunkers down on the idea that you can have your cake and eat it too. Put another way, you can know, understand, *and* use grammar to communicate with humans too! Humor aside, the New View always comes back to the idea that grammar and its constituent elements serve communication. Let's make sure that we understand that by breaking it down just a little bit more in bullet form.

- Most of us use language to do things, i.e., describe a movie we just saw, grow a friendship, or write a term paper on

cell division that sounds like we know what we're talking about.

- To do "language things" requires an ability to use that language.

- To use a language requires the combination and recombination of some set of inputs, i.e., words, sounds, rules, etc. (Remember the *Language Star*?)

- The inputs available to us are governed by rules and regulations. In other words, there is a right and a wrong way to use the inputs, and the rules determine what is correct.

- If we know, understand, and control these rules and inputs, we can construct and use language to get us back to where we started this exploration: to use language to do things.

- Finally, more understanding and control of the inputs and their rules allows us to vary the way we do language. It also allows us to understand the messages of others as they do things with language to and with us.

Reading Comprehension Connection

Just about every reading test ever constructed asks students to analyze a piece of text and to answer comprehension questions. But do we, as expert English language users, ever stop to really look at these passages and overtly ask ourselves what the author is trying to accomplish? In other words, is he or she using language to persuade, to inform, to argue, to explain, to be satirical, and on and on. As English experts, we just seem to get it. We somehow read (probably without effort), understand, and marvel at the author's subtleties, nuances and word plays. We even know sometimes that the author is trying to get us to do something like change our mind, agree with them, or get riled up. But English learners frequently have learned English in less than academic environments that feature a different set of language functions. They know how to talk with friends, chat with family, make a doctor's appointment, and many more tasks. Unfortunately, many of the functions for which they most commonly use English are decidedly non-academic in nature. Certainly, their use of English outside of school accomplishes things, but oftentimes with glaring grammatical errors, pronunciation problems, and breaks in logic and organization. Does the message get communicated? Yes, or probably, or maybe. Does it take the form of erudite grammar usage, skillful word selection, and native-like presentation? Not usually. Functions of language have underlying grammar structures that make them possible. If students lack knowledge of the array of grammar choices available to authors to craft their texts, they are left with few tools or strategies to comprehend. And that can make reading quite difficult.

Academic Writing Connection

The use of functions in writing is as pervasive as it is with reading. From about second grade on, teachers begin to ask students to respond in writing to prompts. Most of those prompts contain a language function—and sometimes more than one. To respond properly requires that students know how to organize language in a way that accurately communicates the function, usually something like comparing, contrasting, defining, or explaining. And they need to use language that sounds academic, authoritative, plaintive, wondering, scientific, and on and on. Without specific instruction in how to use language for academic functions, what choice do they have but to rely on their non-academic language and hope for the best? For example, convincing a person in writing to adopt a different position on an issue is not very similar to the non-academic function of "getting your way." "Give me that pencil!" is a linguistically simple and sometimes very effective way of gaining a writing instrument in second period math. But it does not sound very academic. How about this school task?: *Compare and contrast the Westward Movement in the United States with your own family's historical and contemporary moves.* Try this one: *What should the author have done to elicit more sympathy for the novel's main character?*

To do these tasks in an academic setting requires a knowledge of not only *how* language is used to complete those functions, but *what kinds* of words, tenses, and such could and should be used. Now for the 10,000-dollar question: What language and grammar structures are necessary to produce the language of comparing, contrasting, and consoling? What we need is a method to teach students how to link language functions with language forms, and a powerful one that supports reading comprehension and academic writing. That method is called *Function Junction*.

But beware: its initial simplicity belies its complexity and impact on building English learners who can recognize an author's language manipulations in text and who can make skillful grammar choices that effectively respond to academic-style writing prompts.

Students need practice with recognizing, understanding, and applying specific language structures that relate to both academic and non-academic scenarios that make use of certain language functions.

Method

Function Junction

Description

This method presents students with a typical scenario they are likely to experience. With teacher guidance, students generate an appropriate response to complete the language function.

Purpose

Certain social situations and academic prompts require language users to select and use particular language structures appropriate for that context. The purpose of this method is to have students decipher which language function they are being asked to use and then to complete that function using task-correct grammar skills. Different language functions could include making a request, asking for help, soliciting information, or convincing someone to see an issue your way. Each of these functions requires the use and control of certain language structures; for example, certain verb tenses, modals, or subject pronouns. While English learners generally have one way to complete each language function, native speakers control many and choose them based on their audience, context, and desired outcome. This method helps students to acquire a variety of responses for each language function and to practice them in a relatable scenario.

Materials Needed

- ☐ scenario to present to students
- ☐ chart paper
- ☐ markers

Teacher Skills

- ✓ knowledge of language functions
- ✓ knowledge of levels of formality in language
- ✓ knowledge of use of modals, verb tenses, and other linguistic features relevant to language functions
- ✓ ability to manage students' oral participation and link it to real-life situations

Language Objective: Given a scenario, we will produce questions or statements to complete the language function.

Steps

This method can be done independently of other methods and in any content area. Students complete the method orally but can be assessed either orally or in writing. The steps for *Function Junction* are listed below and fully discussed thereafter.

Function Junction - Steps at a Glance

Preparation	*Procedures*
1. Think of a scenario to present to students.	1. Teacher presents students with a scenario.
2. Prepare the chart.	2. Students identify the language function.
3. Prepare possible responses.	3. Students think of possible responses to complete the language function.
4. Consider response rankings.	
5. Prepare at least one oral practice routine.	4. Students share their responses with a partner and then the whole class.
	5. Teacher records answers.
	6. Teacher guides students to different responses.
	7. Rank responses.
	8. Oral practice.

Discussion of Steps

Before the lesson begins

Step 1-Think of a scenario to present to students.

This first step will direct the lesson. In choosing a scenario to present to students, consider the following:

- What do students need practice saying or writing?
- As a teacher, what are you tired of hearing or reading?
- Which language functions have they already practiced?

Many teachers use *Function Junction* to combat overused or misused language in the classroom. Perhaps students ask to use the restroom incorrectly or incompletely ("Bathroom?") or maybe they need to learn more appropriate ways to ask for their teacher's attention (instead of "teacher, teacher"). Whatever the case may be, there are many language functions for students to practice and learn. Below is a list of commonly used language functions along with polite beginnings.

Language Function	Example	Polite Beginnings
Ask for help	*Could you help me find my homework?*	Excuse me, Excuse me ____(name)__,
Ask for permission	*May I go to recess?*	Pardon me,
Make a request	*Would you please come here?*	Please,
Seek information	*Where is the office?*	May I (or we),
Disagree	*I don't think that's the right answer.*	Would Could
Say "no"	*No thank you.*	Might
Apologize	*I am sorry for losing your pencil.*	Can Should
Offer help	*I would like to help you pick up the trash.*	I would like...
Give advice	*Maybe you should look in the dictionary.*	
Give a warning	*Watch out for the puddle!*	
Make a demand	*Return the book now.*	
Compare ideas	*Both shapes are round.*	
Contrast ideas	*One shape is tall, but the other is short.*	
Make a proposal	*Let's work together!*	

Step 2-Prepare the chart.

Before the lesson begins, write the scenario at the top of the chart paper. Leave room at the very top to identify the language function. Leave plenty of space below the scenario to record student responses.

The chart should now look like this.

> *function*: _____
>
> **You forgot your homework at your house
> and would like to turn it in tomorrow.
> What can you say to your teacher?**

Step 3- Prepare possible responses.

So that you are prepared and can anticipate student responses and guide students to appropriate answers, write some possible responses in your lesson plans. Think about the ideal response that you would like students to use.

Step 4- Consider response rankings.

A "push" for *Function Junction* is having students rank the responses in order of formality. For example, asking, "Excuse me, teacher. May I please get a drink of water?" is more formal and polite than saying, "I'm thirsty. I want some water." Teaching students which responses are more polite and formal helps them to know when to use certain language.

Before the lesson begins, think about how you would like students to rank their responses and when each might be useful. Be prepared to guide students to or teach more formal language.

Step 5- Prepare at least one oral practice routine.

Once students have generated possible responses, how will they practice their responses to simulate real-life conversation as much as possible? Have at least one oral practice procedure ready. Listed below are some possibilities.

- After students have shared their responses, ask students to role-play their conversation in front of the class.
- Have students move down a line or around a wheel sharing their responses.
- Change the intended audience for students and have them change their responses based on the appropriate formality.

During the Lesson

Step 1- Teacher presents students with a scenario.

Explain the scenario to students. Assure that they understand the task.

Step 2- Students identify the language function.

Ask students to consider what the scenario requires that they do. Often key words will be embedded in the scenario. Highlight any key words or features and write the language function at the top of the chart. For beginning level students, the teacher can provide the language function.

Step 3- Students think of possible responses to complete the language function.

Ask students to silently think about how they would complete the language function.

Step 4- Students share their responses with partners.

Allow students time to orally practice their responses with a classmate before calling on a few students to share in front of the whole class.

Step 5- Teacher records answers.

As students generate appropriate responses, write them below the scenario on the chart paper. Try to record a variety of responses.

The chart should now look like this.

> ### *function*: <u>make a request</u>
> ## You forgot your homework at your house and would like to turn it in tomorrow.
> ## What can you say to your teacher?
>
> Can I bring my homework tomorrow?
> Excuse me, Ms. _____, I forgot my homework.
> Can I turn it in tomorrow?
> Would you please let me turn in my homework tomorrow?
> I forgot my homework. I would like to turn it in tomorrow.
> Please excuse me for forgetting my homework.
> May I please turn it in tomorrow?

<u>Step 6- Teacher guides students to different responses.</u>

Students will likely be able to generate two to three different responses on their own. When they have exhausted the possibilities they already know, teach them some other ways to respond by providing prompts such as, "A very polite way to make a request is to start with, 'Would you please let me...' How can you use that to make a request?"

Use your prepared responses to guide students. Provide them with time to think and share with a partner.

Step 7- Rank Responses.

Now that students have generated and practiced a variety of responses, help students to see which responses are most formal and most polite. Help students look for niceties like *please, excuse me, pardon me*, etc. Lead students in a discussion about how you might rank the responses. Assign numbers to the responses with 1 being the most formal or polite.

The chart should now look like this.

---

function: <u>make a request</u>

You forgot your homework at your house and would like to turn it in tomorrow. What can you say to your teacher?

Can I bring my homework tomorrow? **5**

Excuse me, Ms. _____, I forgot my homework. Can I turn it in tomorrow? **2**

Would you please let me turn in my homework tomorrow? **3**

I forgot my homework. I would like to turn it in tomorrow. **4**

Please excuse me for forgetting my homework. May I please turn it in tomorrow? **1**

Step 8- Oral practice

Once students have ranked the responses and know which are the most polite, provide them with an opportunity to role-play the scenario and practice their responses. Make sure that students practice playing both the person completing the language function and the person on the other side of the conversation. Now is a great time to also practice stance, eye contact, and volume. The goal is to simulate a real life scenario as much as possible.

Assessment

Student proficiency for completing language functions can be assessed in the following ways:

- ✓ Students are presented with a scenario and must write their response.
- ✓ Students are presented with a variety of responses for the same language function and must rank them in order of formality.
- ✓ Students role play their scenar
- ✓ ios in front of the class and are graded for giving an oral presentation.
- ✓ Students report on the response given by another classmate and justify or disagree with why that response was chosen.

What *Function Junction* looks like across the language levels

Function Junction can be completed with any language level. However, there are several components that will vary depending on student proficiency.

component/level	Beginner	Intermediate	Advanced
functions	-ask for help -ask for permission -make a request -seek information	-ask for help -ask for permission -make a request -seek information -disagree -say "no" -apologize -offer help	-any
topic	-basic needs -school scenarios	-basic needs -school scenarios -academic discussion	-academic discussion -essay prompts
oral practice	-share with a partner -share in front of the class	-share with partners -share in front of the class -report on what a partner said	-any

What this Method *Isn't*

It's <u>not</u> independent practice. Students are not simply presented with a scenario and then asked for their responses. The teacher has a unique opportunity to train students in appropriate responses that students may not know yet.

It's <u>not</u> a simple repetition or read aloud. Once students have selected their response, they should role-play that response with another person, practicing intonation, stance and volume. Simply reading the written response off the chart paper does not prepare students for real-time conversation.

It's <u>not</u> done in isolation. To simulate real life conversation and decision-making, students must listen to each other and report on what others say. If students are only talking to the teacher, they miss authentic conversation opportunities.

Things to Re-think

1. Can you select a language function (apologizing, whining, asking for a college entrance deferment, or think of another one) and list the language parts and skills necessary to accomplish that task?
2. Do dialogues serve the same purpose as *Function Junction*?
3. The path of least resistance is a popular language operating principle for many English learners, and especially for long-term English learners whose language skills have fossilized. How does this method serve as the antidote to such thinking and its related behaviors?
4. What might a true defender of *communicative approaches* to foreign language instruction say about this method? What would a true defender of the Old View grammar school say?
5. Teachers frequently assign more writing to help English learners to become better writers. Does this make sense in the absence of targeted grammar instruction related to academic language functions?

Administrators' Corner

<u>What to look for in *Function Junction*</u>

➔ Is the method clearly labeled?

➔ Is there a scenario clearly written on chart paper?

➔ Is the language function clearly labeled?

➔ Are there a variety of student responses recorded below?

➔ Do students orally practice their responses before they are written?

➔ Are responses ranked by formality?

➔ Are students provided with time to role-play the scenario with each other?

What to Expect

> Your students have lived for many years using a single—and simple—way of solving a communication problem. They have written the same sentences hundreds of times. They are very skilled at answering questions with the fewest words possible. They are accustomed to teachers finishing their sentences for them. Be prepared to have to de-bunk all of their tendencies toward the path of least linguistic resistance.

> Don't be disappointed initially when students react with minimal delight to learn that there are a myriad of ways to respond to a language prompt.

> They may try to game the method. If you ask for an additional way to say something, and you have already written this on the chart…

>> *"Excuse me sir, I was wondering if you have the correct time."*

> …they may try to get off the hook for thinking and using new language structures through a simple inversion scam:

>> *Sir, excuse me, I was wondering…*

> They will laugh. Use this to your advantage if the situation warrants. These are new sounds, words, patterns, and constructions that will strike them as probably funny, odd, even bizarre. Stand your ground.

> With older students, push toward functions that confront them daily in academic situations. Move quickly past scenarios that happen out of school to ones that impact their day-to-day school life. Discussing a quiz grade diplomatically with a teacher has more linguistic bang for the buck than how to invite a friend to a party.

Voices from the Classroom

Teaching newcomers at the high school level can be difficult. Often, they enter class with no exposure to English and very little literacy in their first language. It can be challenging to get newcomers to participate when they have so little language. That's what makes Function Junction so beneficial: it accelerates the language development of our newest students by providing them with English practice using very practical experiences that they have daily exposure to. As students gain more and more proficiency, Function Junction scenarios become more complex, and this pushes them to continually grow.

If you are teaching this method to newcomers for the first time, hold the expectation that each student participates regularly. Function Junction is perfect because it forces them out of their comfort zones, while at the same time giving them an accessible way to practice English. –Lisa from Coalinga, CA

The language of choices

Old View

A stubborn aspect of the Old View was that skills learned seemed to rarely transfer to use. A valid criticism of the traditional grammar-based approach was that students knew a lot about language, but could apply few if any of those skills to actual communicative situations. In its most extreme form (the Classical View), students would paradoxically be able to describe rules and other mechanical aspects about a language, but could make no usable links to how humans might use those algorithms to do language things. At a bizarre but conscious level, the goal for students became mastering formulas; end of story.

However, we must not lose sight of the precepts that served as the foundation for these classical grammar-based approaches. First was a belief that language structures—the rules, formulas, and algorithms—are as integral to language as are the multiplication tables to math, the periodic elements to chemistry, or the playbook to football. Simply put, language is a rules-based enterprise, so learn them. Second was a belief that once learned, real-life application would follow. Learn the scales on the piano, then apply those to playing Mozart. Learn the box step first, then dance the tango.

Third, and frequently less discussed in modern classrooms, was that formal language instruction viewed through the Classical lens was seen as good training for the mind; that studying grammar laid the cognitive and linguistic foundation for thinking. By way of analogy, grammar-based language learning was equivalent to a full-body workout, so get up early, put on your sweats, and get ready to work.

Out with the Classical
Toward the late 1970s, as we have discussed, the Classical View came under attack. An "easier" version of gaining mastery over a language emerged. Acquisition was how second language learners would come to master English. This simplified approach was included as part of many state teacher certification programs, and the idea of teaching grammar rules in a certain order largely went out the window, at least in public schools.

Communicative approaches to language teaching and learning constituted a sea change reaction to grammar-based instruction. These communicative approaches, headlined by Tracy Terrell's Natural Approach (1977), kicked grammar-based instruction to the curb in favor of a view of language teaching and learning that adhered to the following principles:

- The goal of language teaching is to help students to communicate messages.

- The content of the message is more important than the form of the message.

- If a listener can understand the message, then the language used served its purpose.

- Attention to structure and grammar rule adherence has little importance; it's the message that counts.

- Syllabi for such an approach should be organized by language functions and themes, e.g., going to the store, ordering food in a restaurant, requesting help, or any other of hundreds of contexts in which language and its various forms are used to communicate.

- At a lesson planning level, the key input elements are high interest topics, low affect among students, and easily understood input (read: comprehensible input).

- Grammar errors by students are steps toward correctness and they should not be corrected by teachers. Proper form will come from repeated exposures.

So where grammar-based approaches were dull, tedious, and required effort, communicative approaches favored light topics of interest to students, a focus on using language, and celebrating the communication of messages. Assessment of such approaches was simple: was the

student able to get the message across in a way that was understandable to a native speaker of the language? Under these parameters then, *Want us authors for to readers use this book as helpful in the teaching.*

New View

Our New View, as you have seen throughout this book, is a hybrid that seeks to unify what have traditionally been viewed as polarities. Our New View marries these two polarities and says, quite simply that:

- Knowing and understanding certain grammar concepts makes for better communication.

- Interesting and useful communication contexts create immediate utility for learned grammar concepts.

- Practicing grammar structures correctly while simultaneously doing real things with language helps students to see grammar's application.

- Perfect practice makes permanent. In other words, learning and doing something correctly the first time is far preferable to repeated instances of doing it the wrong way.

The method you are about to learn will provide you a very clear window into both views.

Reading Comprehension Connection

One defining characteristic of academic text is that it features statements of fact or opinion buttressed by proof, or reasons. Read these two examples and see how authors use particular grammar elements to fortify their contentions.

> *Early automakers set as their main goal the provision of cars that were affordable to the general public, since economic conditions for most people were difficult and high-dollar purchases were unthinkable for all but the wealthy.*

> *Educators in the early 20th century placed great faith in providing all students with at least rudimentary instruction in music because it was widely believed—and Plato said it himself—that music and its patterns helped students to learn logical thinking, in addition to gaining valuable ear training that enabled true enjoyment of the classic composers.*

If we look at these examples from a structural perspective we can see that in both cases the authors provide reasons for their assertions that come after the basic sentence. Simplistically, we could identify such a pattern as something like this: *main point + two reasons*. Why would authors the world over, across different languages and content areas, be so adamant about providing proof for their central assertions? Well, among other reasons, it just sounds more convincing, and a central goal of expository and even narrative text is to convince the reader of something by linking statements and facts. For most of us, this structure is invisible; we just read and understand. Authors can even state the reasons first, followed by the assertions, and we just read along. A version of this same pattern can be heard in any grocery store. *Get us a cart please*, the mother says to the child. *We need a cart to hold our groceries and to give you a place to sit when you get tired.* Note the assertion and the two subsequent reasons.

This simple linguistic interaction shows how language structures convey with them thinking structures. Students with underdeveloped language competence frequently lack knowledge and practice with these structures and their related ways of thinking. For example, English learners frequently confuse assertions with reasons, or fail to grasp the connection between the two, thus missing the main points or drawing incorrect conclusions because of their lack of knowledge or use of these structures. Erroneously, teachers sometimes conclude that the students lack the cognitive ability to think in certain ways. But it would be more accurate to say that they lack the language structures that would allow them to think and reason in ways necessary for schooling. Re-read this last statement many times and you will begin to see the faces of your students. Their thinking ability is reduced because of their lack of language structures necessary for that type of thinking.

Every state and federal reading test asks students to find main points. It is also common testing practice to ask students to identify supporting information for those main points. Grammar knowledge can help students to understand text structure, and we will see in this chapter's method how and why the skillful understanding and use of conjunctions is essential when it comes to many school tasks.

 Academic Writing Connection

As you probably have surmised, the method in this chapter, *This or That*, teaches students to make choices and to support their choices with reasons. By way of grammar, they will learn, understand, and use conjunctions to link their statement with logical supports. Most of us have witnessed the speaking and writing of English learners that provides no reasons, only simply constructed statements that ring hollow when the metric is to sound academic, learned, or expert. Here is an excerpt from an adolescent English learner's essay wherein she is responding to the prompt: How have antibiotics improved people's health?

> *Antibiotics are good for people's health and they cure bad diseases.*

She writes a couple of sentences later…

> *Doctors should give the antibiotics to people who need them and should be good doctors.*

In both of these examples (and many others throughout the 250-word essay), she fails to provide any support for her statements. By so doing, she avoids the linguistic imperative to use subordinating conjunctions, those 40 or so words and phrases that can make the difference between academic and non-academic writing structure. Without these conjunctive tools, she will forever string sentences together yet fail to create a unified piece of academic writing that succinctly states a point and makes a case.

Students need to make choices with language and provide grammatically correct reasons for their choices.

Method

This or That

Description

This method presents students with a simple task that is featured on many language tests: choose between two possibilities and then support the answer with two reasons.

Purpose

English learners often have limited ways of expressing a choice outside of one-word answers and "yes" or "no." By explicitly teaching students how to form answers to the questions they routinely encounter in academic settings, students learn a fairly formulaic way to make a statement and support it with reasons. As students are encouraged to use more complex answer frames, more advanced linguistic features are taught and practiced, thus providing a way of using grammar to express a particular type of thinking.

Materials Needed

- ☐ choice to present to students
- ☐ chart paper
- ☐ markers

Teacher Skills

- ✓ ability to provide students with linguistically appropriate questions and answer frames
- ✓ ability to manage students' oral participation and link it to real-life situations

Language Objective: We will make a choice and give two supporting reasons for our choice.

Steps

This method can be done independently of other methods and in any content area. Students complete the method orally but can be assessed either orally or in writing. The steps for *This or That* are listed below and fully discussed thereafter.

This or That - Steps at a Glance

Preparation	Delivery
1. Think of a choice for students to make.	1. Teacher presents students with a choice.
2. Write the question and answer frame that students will use.	2. Students think of reasons to support one choice.
3. Prepare the chart.	3. Students think of reasons to support the other choice.
4. Prepare possible reasons.	4. Students make a decision.
5. Prepare at least one oral practice routine.	5. Students support their answer with two reasons.
	6. Oral practice

Discussion of Steps

Before the lesson begins

Step 1-Think of a choice for students to make.

This first step will direct the lesson and set the tone for how academic or informal the discussion is. When selecting a topic, consider what language structures students need to practice, what vocabulary they should use and what they are studying in other content areas. Topics can range from basic communication skills to vocabulary that is academic in nature. Consider some of the following options.

basic vocabulary	holiday and seasonal	science	social studies	language arts	math
Do you prefer to eat lunch inside or outside?	Are you dressing up for Halloween?	Would you rather study amphibians or reptiles?	Which of the Presidents would you like to meet?	What might be an alternative ending to the story?	Should you solve a multi-digit math equation without a calculator?
Will you walk home or ride the bus?	Would you like to stay home during vacation or go on a trip?	Would it be more interesting to visit a rainforest or a desert?	Should teenagers be allowed to vote?	Did the main character cause the conflict?	Which method will you use to solve the equation and why?

Step 2-Write the question and answer frame that students will use.

There are several question and answer frames to choose from. Eventually, students should be able to develop their own answers by referring to the question. The question you choose will direct student answers so be clear and consistent. On the following page are some options for question and answer frames.

question	answer
Would you rather…?	I would rather…
Do you prefer…?	I prefer….
Which _____ would you choose?	I would choose…
Given the choice between…, what would you do?	Given the choice, I would…
Are you more…?	I am more…
Have you…?	I have…
Should _____…?	_____should…
Could _____…?	_____could…

Step 3- Prepare the chart.

Before the lesson begins, each chart needs:

- the choice that students must make,
- the answer frame students are to use,
  - (For advanced classes, the answer frame can be collaboratively generated.)
- a t-chart to record possible reasons.

The chart should now look like this.

Would it be more interesting to visit the desert or the rainforest? Give two reasons for your answer.

It would be more interesting to _____ (choice) because _____ (reason 1)___ and ___(reason 2).

desert   rainforest

Step 4- Prepare possible reasons.

So that you are prepared and can anticipate student responses, write down a few possible reasons in your lesson plans. When students are stuck, you will know how to prompt them.

Step 5- Prepare at least one oral practice routine.

Once students have made their choices and have supported them with two reasons, how will they practice their responses to simulate real-life conversation as much as possible? Have at least one oral practice procedure ready. Listed below are some possibilities.

- After students have shared their responses, ask students, "What did he/she choose and why?" Students have to use different language to report on others' choices.
- Have students move down a line or around a wheel sharing their responses.
- After students have shared, ask them which of the reasons they heard from someone else that they would like to add to their own.
- Compare or contrast choices and reasons of two or more students.
- After the class has shared, ask students to write a summary statement showing what the whole class would choose.

During the Lesson

Step 1- Teacher presents students with a choice.

Explain the scenario to students. Assure that they understand the task.

Step 2- Students think of reasons they would support one choice.

Ask students to think about only one of the possibilities. What would be a reason to choose that option? As students respond, the teacher writes key words and phrases under the choice on the t-chart.

Step 3- Students think of reasons to support the other choice.

Ask students to now only think about the other choice. What would be a reason to choose that option? Again, write student answers on the t-chart. This is also an appropriate time for the teacher to add his or her own reasons.

The chart should now look like this.

Would it be more interesting to visit the desert or the rainforest? Give two reasons for your answer.

It would be more interesting to _____ (choice) because _____ (reason 1)___ and ___(reason 2).

desert

rainforest

-can see tortoises, coyotes, and lizards	-explore the tree canopy
-won't be rained on	-lots of rain
-might find mineral deposits	-can see birds, snakes, insects, jaguars
-see the stars clearly	-temperature doesn't change much

Step 4- Students make a choice.

Now that each option has reasons to support it, ask students to consider the options and to silently make a choice between the two.

Step 5- Students support their answers with two reasons.

Once students have made their decision between the two options, ask them to consider the reasons listed. They can select reasons from the list or create one or two of their own. Students now share their complete answer with partners.

Step 6- Oral practice

Now that students have shared their answers with at least one person, they are ready for practice in front of the class. Call on students to share their responses or use one of the oral practice routines previously listed.

Assessment

Student proficiency for making a choice and supporting it can be assessed in the following ways:

- ✓ Students are presented with a choice and write their complete answers.
- ✓ Students present each other with choices.
- ✓ Students present their complete answers in front of the class and are graded for their oral presentation.
- ✓ Students report on the answer choices of one or more of their classmates.
- ✓ Students summarize the preferences of the class.
- ✓ Students provide reasons that someone might disagree with their decision.

What *This or That* looks like across the language levels

This or That can be completed with any language level. However, there are several components that will vary depending on student proficiency.

component/level	Beginner	Intermediate	Advanced
topic	-basic needs (school events, holidays, etc.)	-basic needs and content area	-content area
frames	-Would you rather...?	-Would you rather...? -Do you prefer...? -Which would you choose...?	any
oral practice	-share with a partner -share in front of the class	-share with partners -share in front of the class -report on what a partner said	any

What this Method *Isn't*

It's <u>not</u> independent practice. Students are not simply presented with a choice and then asked to answer—that's what happens during an assessment. This method provides the opportunity for teacher guidance and correction. Work through each step with students, leading and correcting them along the way.

It's <u>not</u> a content-focused method. The objective of the method is still to accelerate student language development. Using language correctly is more important than supporting a choice with factual evidence.

It's <u>not</u> done in isolation. To simulate real life conversation and decision-making, students must listen to each other and report on what others say. If students are only talking to the teacher, they miss authentic conversation opportunities.

Things to Re-think

1. How does this method compare to a more traditional dialogue approach?
2. What evidence have you seen that communicative approaches give students a false view of language?
3. Are communicative approaches capable of producing language users who can do academic work in English?
4. As a teacher, would you rather have a student who is skilled in grammar or one who can express him/herself but who lacks grammar correctness? What are the strengths and weaknesses of each?
5. Is it fair to say that communicative approaches were easier for teachers, and thus their popularity?
6. Does the language-thinking connection expressed in this chapter make sense to you? Why or why not?

Administrators' Corner

<u>What to look for in *This or That*</u>

→ Is the method clearly labeled?

→ Is there a choice clearly written on chart paper?

→ Is there a t-chart showing two options?

→ Is an answer frame either written or prepared for the chart?

→ Are students asked to generate reasons for both options?

→ Is precise vocabulary being utilized in the supporting reasons?

→ Does the question and response frame align with the language level of students in the class?

→ Is each student encouraged to make his or her own decision?

→ Are students able to completely answer the prompt with two supporting reasons?

→ Are students provided with time to practice their questions and answers with each other?

What to Expect

➢ Expect students to struggle—mightily in some cases—with the idea of providing a reason for their answer. Think of it this way: what if you were prohibited from providing reasons for any of your answers? How different would that feel? Now you have an idea of how this plays to students who have provided few reasons that utilize sophisticated grammar structures.

➢ Listen for some students' well-developed sense of tautological reasoning. For example: *I prefer swimming in the ocean because swimming in the ocean is what I like.* As the teacher, you have both a language issue to correct and a thinking concept to address that links to language. This is the heavy lifting of language teaching.

➢ Marvel at how students have adopted *cuz* as their main, only, and favorite conjunction of all time. Consider eliminating that one from use in favor of more academic-sounding conjunctions. Or at least challenge them to use it as the first word in their sentence, followed by their linguistically sophisticated assertions. And, by the way, is it legal to use *because* as the first word in a sentence?

➢ Tune up your ears and really listen. Insist on accuracy, or have them do it again. It is not enough that they simply communicated something. It has to be communicated correctly.

➢ Be creative in your use of scenarios. For example, instead of asking: *Would you like to speak with your counselor or the vice principal about a school problem? Give two reasons.*

Try something like this:

> *Is it preferable that high school students communicate more regularly with their counselor or with their school administrators? Give two reasons for your answer.*

Infusing these methods with more content-based material is an excellent strategy for moving stuck intermediates to a new linguistic place. Try it!

Voices from the Classroom

This or That is a great method that gets our English Learners speaking in complete and sometimes even complex sentences. We have incorporated opinion writing into this ELD method to align with the Common Core standards and it's working well! We've been able to scaffold ELA instruction by getting our ELD students speaking with the assistance of sentence frames. We are hoping to now align this method with argumentation for grades 6-12.

—Mary Jo from Coalinga, CA

Vocabulary

Old View

Arguably the most enduring trait of Old View vocabulary learning methods is for students to learn words and definitions. The logic is linear: new word > learn meaning > use in communication. Broken down further, other tenets are as follows:

- The new word is frequently learned independently, or away, from a sentence-level application.

- Definitions are often expressed in this form: x is _____. For example: A dictionary is a book of words. Dogs are mammals.

- The words selected frequently have or don't have some semantic connection. In other words, students learn all of the words to use in the marketplace, or they learn from a random list.

- The global tenet of this belief is that words are what comprise language. Listen to teachers; they frequently prescribe learning more vocabulary as the linguistic cure-all for English learners and non-English learners alike.

Fast-forward to the language acquisition revolution that began in the late 1970s and, once again, we see a complete reversal of philosophy and practice compared to the classical view. Words, according to this enlightened camp, were all of equal value, meaning that none was more important than another and that no category of words (noun, verb, etc.) had more primacy than any other. Indeed, teaching words by grouping them into categories was discouraged, since it harkened back to the traditional teaching methods. After all, what parent ever first taught their child the vocabulary of the kitchen before moving on to vocabulary of the garage?

Second, this Old View 2.0 held that words could be *acquired* without direct instruction. Learning new words would happen in context as students heard them, said them, wrote them, and read them (listen, speak, read, and write). As for the order of these words—syntax—it would just come along for the ride as words were acquired. Analogized to learning to play the piano, one would listen and plunk random notes on the keyboard until one day they self-organized into a melody.

Another tenet of this view is the idea that English learners can really only learn new words in English for which they already know the word and meaning in their home language. Such a view held that teaching students vocabulary in their first language was a necessary and requisite element for learning vocabulary in English. So, how could students learn words like *division*, *metaphor*, *beaker*, and *colonialism* if they didn't first know the word in their home language? This logic supported the provision of bilingual instruction in many places and in many forms. Unfortunately, that meant that many English learners were not taught English vocabulary.

As a side note, if knowing a word and its meaning in one's home language is necessary for vocabulary learning, then how come so many smart adults can't learn a simple list of 10 words for a college Spanish test? After all, most adults know all of the names of the vegetables in English. It's something to think about as we turn the corner to the New View of vocabulary learning.

New View

A New View of vocabulary learning starts from a different place that looks more like how educated parents approach new word learning with their own children.

Watch educated parents with children about five years old or younger and prepare to witness an interesting approach: no matter what the child touches, the parent immediately identifies the object and then discusses its use. It sounds like this:

"No honey, don't touch those. Those are scissors. Mommy uses scissors for cutting material to make dresses for baby."

Another example from millions:
"Look at the mama kangaroo's tummy. That is a pouch and she uses it to keep the babies warm."

Here are some starting points for looking at vocabulary teaching in a new way.

- We learn a great deal of vocabulary by linking a word to its function, not to its definition. This builds utility into learning the new word right from the start.

- This word-function relationship has various iterations, but the link between the object or idea and its use remain constant.

- This word-function relationship helps learners to understand agency: does the item do the acting or is it acted upon. For example, what is the function of a chair? Are chairs used for sitting, or are they sat upon. In this example, chairs are the recipient of the sitting act, and not the agent that does the sitting.

- These word-function relationships are linguistic representations for different ways of thinking. These ways of thinking are foundational for many reading and writing tasks students are asked to do at school. For example, what are metaphors used for? How about microscopes? What are the characteristics of a democracy?

Reading Comprehension Connection

To read with comprehension requires a multitude of cognitive processes. At the higher end of the spectrum, reading requires us to sometimes make analyses, compare and contrast, separate main ideas from details, and to organize information inductively or deductively. There are many other processes that reading requires of us cognitively. Let's look at one way of thinking that is typical of school text: author's use of analogies. Read this short selection and find the analogy.

> *Feeling groggy, he broke the eggs into the pan and scrambled them quickly, seeing in the pan an image of himself and his fellow soldiers crashing to the ground, parachutes trailing, and running in all directions to escape the scorching gunfire.*

Here is the analogy reduced to its core components: Eggs are to scramble as paratroopers are to combat. It's a literacy device that conjures rich images and relates to some other relationship. Let's try another example. Question: *What is a passport and what is it used for?* Answer: *A passport is used to gain entry into a country where you are not already a citizen.* This vocabulary structure is also a way of thinking: something is required in order for something else to happen. Keys are necessary for unlocking locks, sunshine is necessary for plants to grow, sleep is required for mental recharging. Re-conceptualizing vocabulary teaching to also include "teaching thinking" is a big door to open, but an important concept for seeing what vocabulary instruction can be for English learners and their academic success. So how can we teach English learners something as linguistically and cognitively complex as this?

This chapter describes a method that teaches language structures and ways of thinking. If we want students to be able to deduce conclusions from a list of facts, we have to teach that. If we want students to identify main idea and detail, we have to teach that. The method we address in this chapter is a powerful start in building vocabulary and ways of thinking that are valued and necessary in academic environments. The good news is that the method's simplicity and ease of use is in inverse proportion to its power to teach ways of thinking that are critical for text comprehension.

Academic Writing Connection

Analogies, metaphors, and other stylistic devices are unfortunately not a hallmark of writing produced by the vast majority of English learners, regardless of grade level. Paradoxically, we give them text after text that is full of these linguistic representations of thought and expect them to understand and appreciate them. Then we expect them to incorporate them into their own text production. But without being taught the grammar structures that comprise the neurons of these neat ways of thinking, students revert to habitual and literal ways of expressing knowledge, themes and ideas. Or they blindly insert a memorized analogy or metaphor in the strangest of places, causing the native reader to turn the head like a dog hearing a siren. Let's learn how we can help students to learn ways of thinking that reside in certain linguistic structures that we use for linking words or items to their functions.

Students need to articulate with grammatically correct and precise language the names of various objects, their functions, and their attributes.

Method

Vocabulary Frames

Description

Students identify the names of objects and are then guided in expressing the function of the object or its characteristics. For example, "This is a clock and it is used for telling time," and "You can tell it's a clock because it has an hour hand and a minute hand."

Purpose

Language learners frequently know many nouns, but they are unsure about how to describe their function, or what they do. This method is designed to link their lexical skills to syntax and morphological aspects of language. The method simultaneously teaches ways of thinking that are useful in academic writing.

Materials Needed

- ☐ chart paper/sentence strips for frames
- ☐ index cards for labels
- ☐ markers

Teacher Skills

- ✓ knowledge of different vocabulary frames and their use
- ✓ ability to accelerate students' oral responses
- ✓ ability to maintain a brisk pace during oral practice
- ✓ ability to hear students' oral errors and immediately provide correction

Language Objective:

- We will identify objects and explain their specific functions using a vocabulary frame.

- We will identify objects and explain their characteristics using a vocabulary frame.

Steps

This method can be done independently of other methods and in any content area. Students complete the method orally but can be assessed either orally or in writing. The steps for *Vocabulary Frames* are listed below and are fully discussed thereafter.

Vocabulary Frames - Steps at a Glance

Preparation	*Procedures*

<table>
<tr>
<td>

1. Select three to five vocabulary words.

2. Create a label for the object or a picture of the object. You might actually have the object.

3. Select a frame/frames for each vocabulary word.

   *First time: Create the list of frames.

4. Write an explanation for each vocabulary word.

</td>
<td>

1. Teacher presents either the label or the object to students.

2. Students identify object.

3. Teacher asks frame.

4. Students share their responses with a partner.

5. Teacher hears two to three ideas.

6. Teacher provides the explanation that will be used.

7. Students practice the explanation in the specified frame.

8. Repeat for other words.

</td>
</tr>
</table>

Discussion of Steps

Before the lesson begins

Step 1-Select three to five vocabulary words.

The first step is to decide which words students will practice for the week. Three to five vocabulary words per week allows for sufficient practice time. Vocabulary words can come from any content area. Beginning language students greatly benefit from classroom vocabulary as they rarely know the names and functions of the objects that surround them daily. A list of 100 classroom vocabulary words is provided on the following pages for reference.

Moving beyond beginning students, vocabulary words can and should be selected from the content area that students are studying.

Step 2-Create a label.

On an index card, write the name of the object. For classroom vocabulary, this label will remain on the object until students know it. If you would like students to practice a word for which you do not have an object, a labeled picture is sufficient.

Step 3- Select a frame/frames.

Students will practice not only identifying the name of the object but will also articulate the item's function or attributes through the use of a frame. A list of frames is provided on the following page.

For the first *Vocabulary Frames* lesson, make sure you have a list of frames that students will be using. Frames can be written:

- on chart paper
- on sentence strips
- on construction paper

Students will be using these frames to construct their vocabulary sentences. Frames should be clear and legible. Most importantly, students should be able to read the frames from where they are sitting.

<u>Step 4- Write a clear explanation for each vocabulary word.</u>

A practical way to keep track of the vocabulary word and explanation, the function or characteristics of the object, is to write the intended explanation on the backside of the vocabulary label. As you show the vocabulary word to students, you will be reminded of the desired explanation.

In planning the explanation for each vocabulary word, consider which frames you would like students to use and what type of language you would like them to employ. Below is an example.

Word	**Explanation**
atlas	For locating specific places and studying maps, one uses an atlas.

Vocabulary Frames

1.   This/That is a/an _____ and it is used to _____.

2.   This/That is a/an _____ and it is used for _____ing.

3.   These/Those are _____ and they are used to _____.

4.   These/Those are _____ and they are used for _____ing.

5.   To _____, you use a/an _____.

6.   For _____ing, one uses a/an _____.

7.   This/That is definitely a /an_____ because of its _____.

8.   In order to _____, you would make use of a/an _____.

9.   For _____ing, one would employ a/an _____.

10.   You can tell it's a/an _____ because it has a/an _____.

11.   To _____, one will most likely use a/an _____.

12.   Because of its/his/her _____, that/he/she is certainly a/an _____.

13.   Because it possesses _____, one can deduce that it is a/an _____.

14.   One could deduce that this/that is a/an _____, since it has the characteristics of
       _____.

15.   You use a/an _____ to/for _____, but you use a/an _____
       to/for _____.

Tip!

Challenge!

To push students, any of the frames can be used to describe more than one vocabulary word by adding a conjunction of contrast. For example, "That is a minute hand and it used to count the minutes on a clock, **whereas** the second hand is used to count the seconds."

Classroom Vocabulary Words

1. Clock (analog or digital)
2. Minute hand
3. Second hand
4. Electrical outlet
5. Cord
6. Plug (prongs)
7. Telephone receiver
8. Window pane
9. Window latch
10. Window screen
11. Blinds/Curtains
12. Bulletin board
13. Whiteboard
14. Lined paper
15. Chart paper
16. Page
17. Construction paper
18. Graph paper
19. Paper towel
20. Tissue
21. Ceiling
22. Carpet
23. Fire alarm
24. Fire extinguisher
25. Projector
26. Screen
27. Map
28. Globe
29. Vent
30. Cabinet
31. Counter
32. Sink
33. Faucet
34. Cupboard
35. Soap dispenser
36. Paper towel dispenser
37. Speaker
38. Door handle/Door knob
39. Hinges
40. Lock
41. Doorstop
42. Doormat
43. Threshold
44. Calculator
45. Keyboard
46. Monitor
47. Printer
48. Mouse
49. Laptop
50. Legs (chair, desk, or table)
51. Swivel chair
52. Lever (on chair)
53. Cushion
54. Seat
55. Backrest
56. Stapler
57. Staple
58. Paperclip
59. Tape
60. Easel
61. Magnet
62. Shelves
63. Bookcase
64. Atlas
65. Dictionary
66. Thesaurus
67. Journal
68. Folder
69. Binder
70. Notebook
71. Yardstick
72. Podium
73. Flag
74. Schedule
75. Calendar
76. Rules
77. Desk
78. Drawer
79. Handle
80. Tray (whiteboard, desk, or keyboard)
81. Backpack
82. Zipper
83. Filing cabinet
84. File
85. Envelope
86. Stamp
87. Motion detector
88. Sprinkler
89. Fluorescent lights
90. Light bulb
91. Rubber band
92. Note card
93. Sticky note (Post-it)
94. Glue
95. Three-hole punch
96. Basket
97. Roster
98. Light switch
99. Thermostat
100. Photographs

During the Lesson

Step 1- Teacher presents the label or the object to the students.

As you show students the label or the object, you are assessing how many students can readily identify the object.

Step 2- Students identify the object.

See if students can either point out the object or name it. This step will inform you as to how much teaching you will have to do about the object. Responses should sound like, "That is an atlas."

Step 3- Teacher presents frame.

With the object or its label, show students which frame you will have them use to express the object's function. Point out the frame and ask the relating question to students.

Example: What does one use an atlas for?

After asking the question, show students which frame you would like them to use. Students now practice just the frame without the word or function.

Example: For _____(ing), one uses a/an _____.

Ensure that students know where the vocabulary word fits in the frame before moving on.

Step 4- Students share their responses with partners.

Direct students to use the assigned frame to answer your question. Students now practice their sentences with partners.

Step 5- Teacher hears two or three ideas.

Have a few students share their responses using the assigned frame. Affirm or correct responses as

> **Tip!**
>
> **Can we use a student response?**
> Absolutely! By having an explanation for the vocabulary word prepared, you know the level at which you would like students to produce. If a student independently suggests your explanation, a similar explanation, or an even more advanced explanation than what you had prepared, feel free to use it as the class explanation for the word.

students share. You are still assessing what they already know about the object.

Step 6- Teacher provides the explanation that will be used.

After you have heard a few responses from students, provide students with the exact sentence that they will be using. Use the prepared explanation as a reference.

Step 7- Students practice the class explanation and sentence.

With partners, students now practice naming both the object and its function or characteristics in the specified frame. Call on three to five students and ask them the same question from before ("What does one use an atlas for?") while directing them to use the frame.

Tip!

Is it necessary for students to use the exact same sentence?

Students are directed to use the class explanation and the same frame to reduce the number of errors possible. The goal in *Vocabulary Frames* is not only to name objects but also to articulate their function or attributes using the correct grammar.   In using the same sentence, the teacher can focus on a more limited number of possible syntactical and morphological errors.

However, as students advance and have a better command of language, they can produce responses more independently and frames that reflect more complex thinking processes.

Step 8- Repeat the same procedure for other words and explanations.

Depending on the students' language level, you can either introduce a new word and a new frame or only one of those. Repeat the same procedure for the remaining vocabulary words.

Assessment

Student proficiency for identifying vocabulary words and their functions and attributes can be assessed in the following ways:

- ✓ Students are shown an object and must identify it using a vocabulary frame. Students write their responses.
- ✓ Students participate in a "lightning round" of *Vocabulary Frames.* In a given time period (one to two minutes), the class sees how many vocabulary objects they can identify using the vocabulary frames.
- ✓ Students are provided with the explanation for a word and must write the word and label the object.
- ✓ Students are given several vocabulary labels and must correctly place them.
- ✓ Students use vocabulary frames for their oral presentations.

What *Vocabulary Frames* looks like across the language levels

Vocabulary Frames can be completed with any language level. However, there are several components that will vary depending on student proficiency.

component/level	Beginner	Intermediate	Advanced
frames	1-5	1-10	1-15
vocabulary word topics	-classroom - home -school campus -neighborhood -community	content area	content area
number of vocabulary words	two-three/week	three-five/week	five or more/week

What this Method *Isn't*

It's not independent practice. Students are not simply naming objects and using the first definition that comes to mind. This method provides the teacher with an opportunity not only to push students to use more sophisticated language, but to also assure that students use *correct* grammar.

It's not solely focused on semantics, or the meaning of the word. While identifying the correct meaning of the word is important, *Vocabulary Frames* stands out from other vocabulary teaching strategies in that students are asked to use the word in a sentence in which they name its function or characteristics. Correct syntax is equally important in this method as students are once again required to communicate at the sentence level.

It's not a drawn out vocabulary lesson. This method is meant to be brief. Teachers should spend less than five minutes on each word. Students practice the word and its function orally and routinely. This is not the time to discuss all possible meanings of the word and uses for the object. Rather, focus on helping students correctly articulate the object and its function using the assigned frame.

Things to Re-think

1. Is it really possible for a method as seemingly simple as this to teach ways of thinking that students will need at advanced grade levels?

2. What if content teachers used this approach to teaching vocabulary?

3. Is it better to think of this method as superior to the word-definition approach or as an addition to that approach?

Administrators' Corner

What to look for in *Vocabulary Frames*

➔ Is the method clearly labeled?

➔ Are the vocabulary words clearly labeled in the classroom?

➔ Are the vocabulary frames posted for all students to see?

➔ Do students practice their responses with a partner?

➔ Are students directed to use the same vocabulary frame and class explanation?

➔ Does the teacher insist on grammatical accuracy and clear pronunciation?

---

4. Where did educated parents learn this *word-function* method for their own children? Did they all take the same class?

5. Imagine you want to learn more Japanese vocabulary. Would this method work for you?

What to Expect

> Students may find your insistence on accuracy—both of grammar structure and pronunciation—a bit tedious at first. Explain your rationale.

> You may be shocked when you learn, or re-learn, that even English learners with five or more years of so-called English language development instruction cannot name basic items in a classroom. And when it comes to the function or use of those items, hang on to your hat when you learn that producing language in this way is completely foreign (no pun intended) to them.

> In every classroom, there are hundreds—maybe thousands—of items that have particular functions. From door hinges to ceiling tiles to window frames, you could use this method for days and weeks on end and never run out of items to plug into the frames. Walk into a science classroom, or a gymnasium, or a kitchen and the list of items to identify and name their functions starts anew. And what about big concepts from other content areas? Try *theocracy, condensation, estimating,* and literally hundreds of others.

> You may want to laugh—sometimes a little and sometimes a lot—when you hear the funny ways English learners phrase things. When a student suggests that rulers are used for rulering, or that light switches are for lighting, or that globes are for being the world, go ahead and enjoy the moment. You will know then that this method is one they have needed since day one.

Voices from the Classroom

This method really allowed me to focus in on the small parts of everyday language that my students needed to be aware of. It was great not only for working on singular and plural rules, but also for using precise language. As my students language progressed, I was able to make the frames more oriented towards other academic content areas, which really gave them an advantage when they were in their core classes. -Stacy from Le Grand, CA

Synonyms

Think about the number of synonyms you know. It's a difficult concept to grasp and a task you have not likely tried to do. Most educated native speakers have a large inventory of synonyms. But why? Because knowing more than one word for an idea or object allows us to select the one that works best for the meaning we want, or that fits within a syntax pattern we control. At another level, we use synonyms to impress, to bamboozle, to be amusing, and for a host of other reasons. For English learners, however, synonyms are frequently far down the priority list for a simple reason: they have learned that knowing one word to represent something is much easier. And much of their schooling has permitted—indeed advocated—just such an approach. Let's look at two different views of synonym teaching.

Old View

The dominant idea in the Old View is that all words for a particular thing or idea are about equal in value. For example, if a student knows the word "house," that is a good catchall word that works for a variety of living quarters, e.g. shack, shanty, mansion, or flat. Here are other highlights of this view.

- Synonyms will be learned "in context." Of course, the word "context" is rarely defined, but it can generally be interpreted as "while reading." Thus, as students read, they will build synonym knowledge. Teachers in this view are prone to interrupt student reading to flag a new synonym; then students keep reading and start forgetting the new synonym.

- Synonyms are bonus words; if you know more than one word for something, great! If you don't, keep reading.

- Synonyms are mainly useful for describing. This means that we spend most of our ELD instruction discussing adjective synonyms, but hardly ever synonyms for other parts of speech (What is a synonym for *coincidentally*? How about for *to investigate?*)

- Synonyms can be learned and taught independent of any syntactic rules or semantic implications. Here is a word and here are its synonyms. Commit these to memory and then use them properly, teachers say to students.

New View

A New View of synonyms looks and sounds a bit different. Or should we say,

A fresh perspective on linguistic isomorphs, without a doubt, presents itself differently and resonates altogether dissimilar.

- Synonyms must be taught. Students will not naturally go hunting for new words any more than most adults will. If the word that pops into our heads works, most of us go with it. So students must be taught synonyms explicitly.

- Synonyms should be taught across all parts of speech. To sound academic in writing, the use of verb synonyms packs more punch usually than a boatload of words meaning the same as "big."

- They are not "bonus" words, but rather one iconic way native proficient speakers differentiate themselves from less competent speakers of a language.

- Synonyms should be taught and learned in groups that allow for ranking them in terms of meaning, impact, force, or other criteria. You will see in the method that follows how students are taught to organize words into groups that start with colloquial and build to maximum academic impact.

- Synonyms are only useful to learn if you can use them in a grammatically correct sentence.

- Learning synonyms for known words is one of the fastest ways we have of expanding not only English learners' vocabularies, but our own as well.

Reading Comprehension Connection

Take a moment and read this paragraph.

Coffee has become one of America's leading industries, with your favorite cup of mud available seemingly on every corner just in case your urge for brew overwhelms your common sense that tells you 10 cups of joe per week adds up to some serious grounds for re-thinking your caffeine intake.

How many synonyms did the author use for "coffee," and why the variance? Of course, we know that authors try to keep sentences perky and non-repetitive and they use synonyms as a popular tool for accomplishing that. Select any school textbook and read a random paragraph. It is unlikely that you will see the same word used over and over again if there is a workable synonym available. Moreover, authors recognize that, semantically, not all synonyms are created equal. Most teachers during a staff meeting know the same thing when getting ready to air an issue. Depending on the effect one desires, a word choice is made from a menu of options. Using a computer analogy, the search for the right word can be likened to a drop-down computer screen menu. We scan the list at lightning speed, clear the throat, and launch our grievance with just the choice word to describe our sentiment. Some of the options are below:

Mr./Mrs. Principal, your decision to change the afternoon bell schedule by two minutes has me a bit _____.

> miffed
> peeved
> perturbed
> irritated
> riled up
> mad
> irate

Which word choice would you recommend to a new teacher? Which can a veteran teacher get away with? Which would cause the most heads to turn? Whatever your intent, notice that in our native-speaking heads, the drop-down menu comes neatly organized semantically so that we can make our best selection.

Proficient users of a language rely on these drop-down synonym lists not only when they speak, but certainly when reading. In fact, reading becomes—in a weird kind of way—a competition we have with the author. Do we have all the words in our drop-down menus that the author uses in the book? English learners, faced with textbooks written by authors with this magic power, silently hope that their one-word drop-down menu—*house*—will be used throughout the reading.

 ## Academic Writing Connection

Here is the paragraph you read above, but this time it is translated into English-learner speak.

Coffee has become one of America's leading industries, with your favorite cup of coffee available on every corner just in case your urge for coffee overwhelms your common sense that tells you 10 cups of coffee per week adds up to some serious coffee for re-thinking your coffee intake.

Are you sick of reading the word *coffee*? How many times last week did you read student writing that was littered with simple words like *cool, nice, fun, interesting,* and *neat* that were used over and over again? If we want students to use synonyms in their writing across all parts of speech, then we need to teach them how to build the drop-down menus that proficient speakers use. More importantly, if English learners are going to sound academic when they write, we need to help them to order their drop-down menus semantically so they can make the best word choice for the task, genre, or author's purpose. Of course, we better start at the beginning, and that means breaking to English learners the bad news: there is more than one way to say *coffee, house,* and *nice.*

> ***Students need*** to understand how synonyms and word choices affect the meaning of a sentence and how to choose the best option for their language production.

Method

Vertical Sentence

Description

In this method, the teacher and students collaboratively generate synonyms for words within a given sentence. Once synonyms are generated, those that work within the context of the sentence are used to form new syntactic and semantic variations of the sentence.

Purpose

To link known words and concepts to new vocabulary that is semantically ranked according to its utility in academic contexts.

Materials Needed

- ☐ sentence
- ☐ chart paper
- ☐ markers
- ☐ *Grammar Wall*

Teacher Skills

- ✓ understanding of synonyms and contextual use
- ✓ understanding of syntactic changes necessary with synonym replacement

Language Objective: We will replace the underlined words with synonyms that do not change the meaning of the sentence.

Steps

This method can be done independently of other methods and in any content area. However, in completing this method, students benefit from having already practiced both *Verb Tense Study* and *Syntax Surgery*. The steps for *Vertical Sentence* are listed below and are fully discussed thereafter.

Vertical Sentence - Steps at a Glance

Preparation

1. Select a sentence that has from two to five words that can be replaced with synonyms. Write this sentence on chart paper.

2. Select words to be replaced by synonyms. Underline them.

3. On your lesson plan, prepare a list of possible synonyms for students to use for each word.

4. Prepare the contextual meaning discussion. Which synonyms will work in the sentence? Which won't? Why?

5. On your lesson plan, prepare the sentence that you will use to replace the original.

Procedures

1. Students read sentence aloud.

2. Teacher points out first underlined word and asks students to think of synonyms for that word.

3. Teacher writes words that are synonyms for underlined word below.

4. Repeat the same procedure for each underlined word.

5. Teacher and students collaboratively cross out synonyms that change the meaning of the sentence and have a discussion about contextual meaning.

6. ***Optional "push" step**
   Teacher helps students rank synonyms based on meaning or register.

7. Teacher selects replacement words to create a new sentence and writes that sentence below the original.

8. Student practice

Discussion of Steps

Before the lesson begins

Step 1-Select the sentence.

Sentences for *Vertical Sentence* can come from any content area. Use a sentence that has at least two words that students can replace with synonyms. Consider key vocabulary that students are learning. Using the vocabulary word itself or a synonym for that word will encourage students to apply their knowledge of the word's meaning.

When you have selected a sentence, write it on chart paper large enough for the whole class to see. Be sure to leave space between the lines to allow for the vertical synonym replacement. (Remember the drop-down menu analogy?)

Step 2-Select words to be replaced.

Students will practice both the semantics and syntax of the underlined words so choose them wisely. Consider current vocabulary words, targeted parts of speech, and overused words that you would like students to stop using. Underline all words that will be replaced in the sentence.

The chart should now look like this.

During their <u>climb</u>, the <u>nervous</u> <u>backpackers</u>

<u>went up</u> one of the <u>tallest</u> mountains in the

<u>area.</u>

Step 3- Prepare a list of synonyms.

Before the lesson begins, it is essential that the teacher be prepared with a list of possible synonyms for each underlined word. Knowing the synonyms ahead of time allows you to both push students toward certain words and provide students with new words when necessary.

Step 4- Prepare the contextual meaning discussion.

Teachers must not only know a list of synonyms for each word, but must also understand which words fit within the context of the original sentence. Think of yourself as a "living thesaurus." Be prepared to explain to students why certain words can replace the underlined word and why others can't.

> *Tip!*
>
> ### Which sentence and words should I select?
>
> The quality of the selected sentence and underlined words plays a huge part in determining the quality of the *Vertical Sentence* method. Start by thinking about which words or kinds of words you would like students to understand better and use more effectively.
>
> Perhaps your students overuse certain adjectives such as "good" or "happy." Using a *Vertical Sentence* not only introduces new synonyms but also shows students the context in which to use them.
>
> Another way to select sentences and words is to consider the content you are currently studying. If new vocabulary is introduced, *Vertical Sentence* provides a unique opportunity for students to practice both the meaning of the word and its syntactic use in sentences. The vocabulary word can either be one of the underlined words in the sentence—requiring students to explain the meaning—or the underlined word can be a simpler term for the targeted vocabulary word. The latter approach requires students to think of the new word when provided with the meaning.

Step 5- Prepare the replacement sentence.

So that the lesson flows smoothly, prepare the sentence that you will write using replacement synonyms. For example, if the original sentence is *The candidate responded to the absurd questions from the nosy reporter,* the replacement sentence could be *The candidate replied to the ridiculous questions from the prodding reporter.*

During the Lesson

Step 1- Students read the sentence and objective.

In this very brief step, ensure that students can pronounce all the words in the sentence and understand what they will be doing.

Tip!

Watch the morphology!

When listing the synonyms for the underlined words, make sure that the morphology of the words is the same. For example, if the underlined word is "tasks," all listed synonyms should also be in the plural form. The same goes for verb tense. Make sure that the verb tenses for the listed synonyms match that of the underlined words.

Step 2- Generate synonyms for the first underlined word.

The teacher points out the first underlined word and asks students to think of possible synonyms for that word. Students then share their responses with a partner and answer in complete sentences ("A possible synonym for ___ is ___."). This step encourages the behavior of mentally looking for an existing drop-down menu.

Step 3- Teacher writes synonyms below underlined words.

As students generate synonyms, the teacher either validates that the word is a synonym for the underlined word and writes it below, or corrects students by explaining that the given word is not a synonym and does not write the word down. It is essential that *only* synonyms for the word are written on the chart paper. However, all synonyms can be recorded even if they do not fit within the context of the sentence. Think "vertically" for now as context will be addressed later.

If students struggle with generating synonyms, now is the time to introduce and teach new words. The teacher gives a brief explanation of the context of any new words.

<u>Step 4- Repeat the same procedure for each of the underlined words.</u>

Continue to ask students to think of possible synonyms for each underlined word following the same procedure from Step 3.

The chart should now look like this.

During their <u>climb</u>, the <u>nervous</u> <u>backpackers</u>

       ascent   anxious   mountaineers

       rise   agitated   climbers

       take off   distressed hikers

<u>went up</u> one of the <u>tallest</u> mountains

scaled   highest

climbed   biggest

ascended   largest

arose   most elevated

in the <u>area</u>.

   region

   neighborhood

   territory

Step 5- Teacher crosses out synonyms that change the meaning of the sentence.

For this step, the teacher leads a discussion on the context, or particular meaning and area of use, of each listed synonym. As you go through each listed synonym, try replacing the underlined word. Does it change the meaning of the sentence? Why or why not? Explain to students the contextual difference between the synonym and the underlined word as used in the sentence if one cannot replace the other.

The chart should now look like this.

During their <u>climb</u>, the <u>nervous</u> <u>backpackers</u>

ascent	anxious	mountaineers
~~rise~~	agitated	climbers
~~take off~~	distressed	hikers

<u>went up</u> one of the <u>tallest</u> mountains

scaled	highest
climbed	biggest
ascended	largest
~~arose~~	~~most elevated~~

in the <u>area</u>.

region

~~neighborhood~~

territory

Notes on Context

- "Rise" and "take off" have to do more with going up in the air. One does not go up a mountain this way.
- "Neighborhood" is a synonym of "area" but it refers to a place populated by people living in houses or other dwellings, not where one would climb a mountain.

**Optional "push" step*

<u>Step 6- Teacher helps students to rank synonyms by shades of meaning or register.</u>

As a challenge for students, sort the synonyms either by shades of meaning or by register, which has to do with levels of formality. For example, if sorting by shade of meaning, *joyful, glad,* and *ecstatic* are all synonyms for *happy.* However, these words can be sorted by levels of happiness, with the last word showing *happy* to the greatest extent. Thus, the ranking below:

- A. glad
- B. joyful
- C. ecstatic

Explaining to students that synonyms can have different levels helps them to more appropriately select synonyms in the future. The synonyms for the word *nervous* are sorted in this way on the chart on the next page. Another way to sort the synonyms is by register, or the level of formality, between academic and more commonly used words. Consider the words: *to run away, to abscond, to flee.* All three words are synonyms meaning *to depart quickly.* However, they can be sorted by asking students, "Which sounds the most academic?" or "Which is most likely to be seen in academic text?" Through this lens, the words would be sorted in the following way with the third word being the most academic:

1. to run away
2. to flee
3. to abscond

From our chart sample above, using the word *nervous* to discuss shades of meaning and *went up* for register, the words could be ranked as shown on the chart on the following page.

Tip!

How can I help students understand context?
Synonyms are easily found in thesauri. Context is not. As the "living thesaurus," help students understand *why* certain synonyms change the meaning of the sentence and others don't. To help students, you can write key words or phrases or draw quick illustrations next to words to explain their context.

The chart should now look like this.

During their <u>climb</u>, the <u>nervous</u> <u>backpackers</u>

ascent	**B** anxious	mountaineers
~~rise~~	**A** agitated	climbers
~~take off~~	**C** distressed	hikers

<u>went up</u> one of the <u>tallest</u> mountains

1 climbed   highest

2 scaled   biggest

3 ascended   largest

~~arose~~   ~~most elevated~~

in the <u>area</u>.

region

~~neighborhood~~

territory

Step 7- Teacher selects replacement words and writes new sentence.

Using your prepared sentence, show students how you will maintain the meaning of the original sentence while replacing the underlined words with synonyms from the generated lists. Write this sentence at the bottom of the chart.

The chart should now look like this.

During their <u>climb</u>, the <u>nervous</u> <u>backpackers</u>

    ascent   **2** anxious   mountaineers

    ~~rise~~   **1** agitated   climbers

    ~~take off~~   **3** distressed hikers

<u>went up</u> one of the <u>tallest</u> mountains

1 climbed   highest

2 scaled   biggest

3 ascended   largest

~~arose~~   ~~most elevated~~

in the <u>area</u>.

    region

    ~~neighborhood~~

    territory

During their ascent, the anxious climbers scaled one of the largest mountains in the region.

Step 8-Student practice

Have students write their own sentences using synonyms from the list. They can share their sentences orally with a partner first to practice. For an extra challenge, ask students to use different shades of meaning or only academic words.

Assessment

Student proficiency for proper synonym use can be assessed in the following ways:

- ✓ Students independently select synonyms that do not change the meaning of the sentence.
- ✓ Students rank synonyms in order of shades of meaning.
- ✓ Students rank synonyms in order of academic register.
- ✓ Students write their own sentences and underline words to be replaced by a partner.
- ✓ Students do a *Vertical Sentence* in reverse by generating an antonym for each of the underlined words.

What *Vertical Sentence* looks like across the language levels

Vertical Sentence can be completed with any language level. However, there are several components that will vary depending on student proficiency.

component/level	Beginner	Intermediate	Advanced
types of synonyms	-basic vocabulary (common nouns, action verbs, adjectives of feeling, size)	-content area vocabulary words (adjectives, nouns, verbs)	-academic vocabulary (adjectives, nouns, verbs, adverbs, conjunctions)
number of synonyms	-two-three	-three-five	-four or more
push	shades of meaning optional	shades of meaning or academic register	shades of meaning or academic register mandatory

What this Method *Isn't*

It's <u>not</u> time to list as many words as possible below each underlined word. The underlined words and accompanying synonyms should be chosen strategically. Remember, *only* synonyms are written on the chart.

It's <u>not</u> a student-led method. If students completely understood synonyms and their contextual use, they would not need to use the *Vertical Sentence* method. This method is facilitated by the teacher as the "living thesaurus."

It's <u>not</u> a thesaurus hunt. While teaching students to use a thesaurus and having them do so independently are valuable lessons, this method is based on collaborative class participation. As the "living thesaurus," the teacher directs the use of synonyms and provides contextual correction.

Things to Re-think

1. Do adults you know memorize lists of synonyms? Why not?
2. If you ever studied a foreign language, do you remember how it felt to learn words—even synonyms—that you could not use in a sentence?
3. This method relies heavily on keeping the synonym learning within actual sentences, versus learning synonyms as isolated words. What would an Old View proponent say about this approach?
4. Brain research suggests that the brain functions more like a sieve than a sponge. If that is true, doesn't this method provide more ways for the words and their meanings to stick and not drift away?

Administrators' Corner

<u>What to look for in *Vertical Sentence*</u>

➔ Is the method clearly labeled?

➔ Is there a sentence clearly written on chart paper?

➔ Are there words underlined in the sentence?

➔ Are synonyms (and only synonyms) listed beneath each underlined word?

➔ Are the synonyms appropriate for the grade level and language level?

➔ Are any of the listed synonyms ranked in some way?

➔ Is there a sample sentence using synonyms written below the original sentence?

➔ Can students explain why certain synonyms are appropriate and others are not?

➔ Do students write their own sentences after the collaborative lesson?

What to Expect

- ➤ Excitement. This form of vocabulary enhancement engages students at many levels. Some students will delight in providing a synonym that no one else knows, while others will be ultra-creative as they index their word repository. The bottom line is that it's a method that captures students' attention because the learning is immediate and they quickly apply their learning at a sentence level.

- ➤ For adolescent-age students at an intermediate or even advanced English level, you might receive a few subtle nods of gratitude and appreciation. After all, they have learned lots of words over the years that have flown loosely around in their brains in the absence of a coherent organizing system. When intermediate proficient and advanced students begin to categorize words in this way, they come to better understand their own linguistic competence, including their strengths and deficiencies.

- ➤ Students will listen longer to your subtle discussions of word meanings because they understand the underlined word and concept you are parsing. Really, they will.

- ➤ Students can get silly with this if you let them. And, of course, this method is not for generating lists of synonyms that have no use or suitability in academic environments.

- ➤ You will be caught flat-footed at some point in your use of this method by a student's suggested synonym. Stop, think about it, and even think out loud for them as you wrestle with its applicability. Semantics (word meaning) can be a slippery slope, even for native speakers.

- ➤ Students will enjoy a spirited debate about what they believe a word to mean. Isn't that a good thing?

- ➤ Don't worry if there is only one synonym for the word you have underlined. Maybe there isn't even one synonym for it. That is a great day for students, and recognition that they do know a lot of words and that many of their drop-down menus are indeed complete. Native speakers and language learners alike can share that great feeling.

> ### Voices from the Classroom
>
> *Vertical Sentence allowed me to teach not only the meaning, but many of the nuances of words. My students enjoyed debating and supporting their word choices with their classmates. I enjoyed creating sentences that related to Social Studies so that the kids could show how much they knew about the topic through their debate.* –Stacy from Le Grand, CA

Morphology

Old View

By now it is probably clear that the oldest of the old views (Classical) has taken a beating over the years, notwithstanding many of its good and enduring qualities. But it is perhaps in the area of morphology where the Classical View has been most vilified and that most accounts for its poor public image. For it is in the zone of morphology where many a frustrated foreign language learner has found himself lost, treading water in the deep, dark sea of language, grasping blindly for a life preserver to save him from the ominous shadow in the water that looks like…another verb tense. "No!" many a stranded Old View language learner has shouted. "Not another verb tense!" And so it went that students learned to conjugate verb after verb after verb, with each new week bringing a new and more difficult and less understood tense to conjugate. The course syllabus was organized by tenses, the book followed suit, and students trudged across campuses carrying the *501 Spanish Verbs* book in hopes that by its portage the information would seep into the veins and be carried to the brain. *Yo tengo, tú tienes, él tiene*…and so it went. By learning verbs and their conjugations, it was believed, the able student would then possess the master key

to grammar, and thus be able (finally) to make glorious use of all those previously memorized vocabulary words in real sentences. Many came to hate verbs, blaming them and their accompanying subject pronouns for the misery they made of their previously happy life.

The pure Classical View and its related methods celebrated other aspects of language morphology, delighting in special word endings that changed according to gender, number (plural vs. singular), and part of speech. Fueled by a belief that big complicated things are best understood by learning their smallest parts and then reassembling them, the Old View embraced morphology, since by design it deals with small units of meaningful language that are embedded (or deliberately hidden) in other words.

New View

There's simply no denying that language relies on morphology for spice and variety. These little units of language mean something when they join together or with an existing word: *walk +ed* becomes walked, *anti + establishment* becomes antiestablishment, and *im* + pure + *ity* becomes a word that is just fun to say. If we are all language masons, morphology

Morph House

comprises the bricks we use to construct our language walls. But unlike finding joy in the simple description of each piece, the New View sees morphology as an energy field laden with little language electrons and protons just waiting to make words sizzle and sparkle. Here are the key points about morphology in the realm of language teaching and learning.

- Affixes and suffixes—the stock-in-trade of morphology—serve to transform words into different parts of speech.

- Most words belong to a word family, that is to say, most words can be represented as more than just one part of speech. For example, *map* is a noun, but *mapped* is a past tense verb.

- There are thousands of word families in English that are constructed by adding morphemes. The meanings of many morphemes are finite; they add a specific many to the words to which they are attached.

- When it comes to verbs, English is pretty stingy on the morphemes: *s, ing, ed*. By understanding the meanings of the morphemes, verbs can be understood, rather than memorized based on form.

- Learning new vocabulary morphologically is more logical and linear than just learning random word lists. Here is the logic demonstrated:

  o Democrat
  o Democrats
  o Democracy
  o Democracies
  o Democratic
  o Democratically
  o To democratize
  o Democratization

Reading Comprehension Connection

Select a passage from a book or text of your choosing. Begin reading anywhere.
Congratulations, you have found the morphemes. This sounds silly, but morphemes are
everywhere in text, and some morphemes show up more regularly than a pesky relative around
the holidays. Unfortunately, most non-grammar-enlightened English learners approach text as
a word-by-word exercise. They look at a word; if it is known and understood, they move to the
next word and repeat the process. When they come across unknown words, though, they
frequently find themselves stuck in a binary world of either knowing it or not. They
unfortunately possess little in the way of overt grammar knowledge that could be applied to
making sense of the word or of recognizing its relative importance or function in the sentence.

A morphological perspective of reading comprehension holds that language learners need to
look at the text for known morphological characteristics. In which verb tense is the sentence
written? How do I know that? What language function does this morphological construction
play? Is there a spelling pattern that represents a morpheme I have seen before and can link
to a part of speech from the Grammar Wall? These and other types of questions are what help
English learners to use their developing grammar knowledge and control in the service of
reading comprehension. It usually doesn't take long for a grammar-savvy student to realize
that the paragraphs on cell division tend to use the base word *divide* in a lot of different
morphological forms: *divided, division, dividing, undivided, divisible*. The meaning of the
various word family members stays about the same, but the word's function in the sentence is
marked by the morpheme it is wearing. That is enlightenment that leads to understanding.

Academic Writing Connection

It must be difficult to write a persuasive paragraph on the importance of friendship when the
only words you really can control within a sentence are *friend* or *friends*. Let's try it so that we
can experience what many experienced English learners confront on a daily basis in academic
situations where they lack knowledge of morphological word families. Here goes...

*Friends are important to almost all people. Having a friend can help you when you are sad
or having problems. A good friend can support you when you feel down or mad. Friends
help you to enjoy life better too. Your friend can join you for fun activities, or a friend can
meet your other friends and then you can all be friends. Almost everyone needs one or two
good friends. Everyone should also be a friend to others.*

You get the idea. *Friend* and *friends* are only two members of the *friend* family. Other members of the family come from different places on your *Grammar Wall*. From left to right across the parts of speech: *friendship, to befriend, to de-friend* (thank you, social media), *friendly, unfriendly, friendless and friendlessness*. With all these choices available to the grammar-instructed student, the essay takes on a different form. Teach this student 100 more word families, along with some solid verb tense control, and she is on her way to having a pretty good foundational arsenal for academic writing. And along the way, she realizes that learning English does not equate to having to memorize every word in the English language. Instead, she strategically uses a select inventory of morphemes that allows her to construct sentences in very different ways and that have a decidedly more academic tone and presentation. So let's now learn about how to help our students with this exciting aspect of language known as morphology.

Students need to understand how prefixes and suffixes change a base word into different parts of speech, each with its own place in the syntax system and each with a similar but distinct meaning.

Method

Morph House

Description

The teacher assists students to build a morphological word family from a base word. Students are then guided to use the derivatives, or words that can be generated from the base word, in sentences and to identify the part of speech for each.

Purpose

This method directly teaches how to add morphemes to base words to create word families that are then used in sentences.

Materials Needed

- ☐ chart paper
- ☐ markers

Teacher Skills

- ✓ knowledge of base words and derivatives
- ✓ knowledge of affixes and their meaning and use
- ✓ knowledge of syntax rules

Language Objective: We will generate words from the same base word, use each new word in a complete sentence, and identify the part of speech of each new word based on its form, function, and syntax.

Steps

This method can be done independently of other methods but students would benefit from having already practiced both *Verb Tense Study* and *Syntax Surgery*. The teacher guides students through a collaborative chart and students write sentences independently. The steps are listed below and are fully discussed on the following pages.

Morph House - Steps at a Glance

Preparation	**Procedures**
1. Select the base word and derivatives.	1. Teacher presents the chart and base word to students.
2. Prepare the lesson plan.	2. Students generate derivatives from base word.
3. Prepare the chart.	3. Students generate a sentence for each base word.
	4. Students identify parts of speech.
	5. Independent practice.

Discussion of Steps

Before the lesson begins

Step 1-Select the base word and derivatives.

In selecting a word for *Morph House*, consider students' vocabulary words, spelling words, or frequently misused words. Choose a word that has at least three derivatives that would benefit students in an academic environment. A list of commonly used base words and derivatives is provided in this chapter for your reference.

Step 2-Prepare the lesson plan.

With the base word and derivatives chosen, think about the sample sentences that you would like students to write and which parts of speech you would like them to use. A sample lesson plan is provided below. Blank lesson plans follow the table of base words and derivatives

Morph House Lesson Plan	word: plant (v.)	definition: to put in the ground for growth	derivatives: plants, planted, planting, planter
derivative	*parts of speech*	*sample sentence*	*part of speech clues*
plants	(noun) verb	Aquatic plants grow underwater.	-plants = subject -precedes verb (grow) -names a thing
planted	verb, (adjective)	The planted flower has grown six inches!	-planted describes flower -precedes a noun -ends in "ed"
planting	noun, (verb) adjective	The gardener was planting the bulbs while removing the dead flowers.	-to be verb + verb-ing -after subject (the gardener) -subject does action of verb
planter	noun	The students replaced the soil in the planter.	-ends in "er" -after "the" (article) -names a thing

For each derivative that students will use, consider which part(s) of speech the word could be. Often, a word can be more than one part of speech depending on its use. Decide which part of speech you would like students to use. Also think about what clues will help students identify different parts of speech. The illustration below shows students the aspects of a word in a sentence that helps to determine its part of speech.

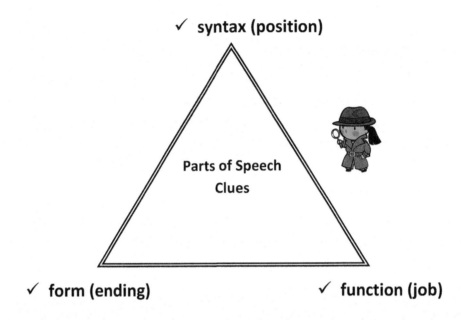

During the lesson you will direct students to consider three criteria when identifying parts of speech: function (job), suffix/ending (form), and syntax (position). If you've been practicing other methods like *Syntax Surgery*, you already have two sets of clues in your classroom. The functions of parts of speech can be found on the definition placards on your *Grammar Wall*. The syntax for different parts of speech should be posted with your syntax rules (See chapter on *Syntax Surgery*.). The final set of clues—suffixes or common endings (form)—can be found below. Provide the common endings chart for students or add the suffixes to your *Grammar Wall*.

Common Endings			
adjectives	**nouns**	**verbs**	**adverbs**
• able	• tion	• ing	• ly
• ive	• ence/ance	• ed	
• ic	• y	• s/es	
• y	• ing		
• ing	• al		
• ed	• ment		
	• ness		
	• er/or		

base word	derivatives
Basic Vocabulary	
bake	baker, baked, baking, baked
create	creator, created, creates, creating, creative, creation
decorate	decorator, decorative, decorates, decorating, decorated
heat	heater, heated, heats, heating, heatedly, preheat, reheat
help	helper, helps, helped, helping, helpful, helpless
plant	planter, plants, planted, planting
work	worker, works, worked, working
Language Arts	
analyze	analysis, analyzed, analyzing, analyzes
character	characterize, characterization, characteristically, uncharacteristically
develop	developer, developing, develops, developed, development
evaluate	evaluator, evaluates, evaluated, evaluating, evaluative
inspire	inspires, inspired, inspiring, inspiration
organize	organizer, organizes, organized, organizing, organization, disorganized
reflect	reflects, reflecting, reflected, reflection, reflective
Math	
add	adds, added, adding, additive, addition, additionally
compare	compares, compared, comparing, comparison, comparative, comparatively
divide	divides, divided, divisor, dividing, dividend, division
increase	increases, increased, increasing, increasingly
measure	measures, measuring, measured, measurement, measureable
multiply	multiplies, multiplied, multiplying, multiplication, multiple
transfer	transfers, transferred, transferring
Science	
accelerate	accelerates, accelerated, accelerating, accelerator, acceleration
decompose	decomposes, decomposed, decomposing, decomposer, decomposition
habitat	inhabitant, inhabitable, habitable, habitation
live	lives, lived, living, livable, lively
observe	observes, observed, observing, observer, observable, observation, observatory
rotate	rotates, rotated, rotating, rotation
supply	supplies, supplied, supplying, supplier
Social Science	
argue	argues, argued, arguing, arguable, arguably, argument
complete	completes, completed, completing, completely, completion, incomplete
judge	judges, judged, judging, judgment, misjudge
manage	manages, managed, managing, manager, management
migrate	migrates, migrated, migrating, migration, immigrate, emigrate, migratory
populate	populates, populated, populating, population
produce	produces, produced, producing, producer, production, productive
prove	proves, proved, proving, provable, proof, proven
vote	votes, voted, voting, voter

Step 3- Prepare the chart.

Draw the outline of a house on a piece of chart paper. The base word and its definition will go in the "attic" and the derivatives and sentences will be written below. You can pencil in your notes directly on the chart as well. Depending on students' age and language ability, they can also follow along on their own *Morph House* worksheet. A blank sample is provided on the following page.

The chart should now look like this.

to plant (v.)

Tip!

Affix Chimney

For beginning students, younger students, or students doing the method for the first time, consider providing the affixes (prefixes and suffixes) that you would like for them to use. One way to do so is to add a "chimney" to the house where the affixes reside.

Name: _____

Morph House

1. _____

2. _____

3. _____

4. _____

During the Lesson

Step 1- Teacher presents the chart and base word to students.

To begin the lesson, go over the method objective and chart and introduce the base word and definition. Assure that students understand the meaning of the base word.

Step 2- Students generate derivatives from the base word.

Ask students to think about any words that they know that come from the base word. After thinking, they share their ideas with a partner. The teacher then calls on students to share their responses and writes the words that are derivatives of the base word. This is also the time to give students a new word they don't know and to push them to think of specific parts of speech.

Tip!

How many derivatives go on the chart?
Four to five derivatives is sufficient, but you will be limited by space on the chart and time in the lesson. If students generate more derivatives than you would like to write on the chart, affirm their responses but let them know that they will be studying other words for the lesson.

The chart should now look like this.

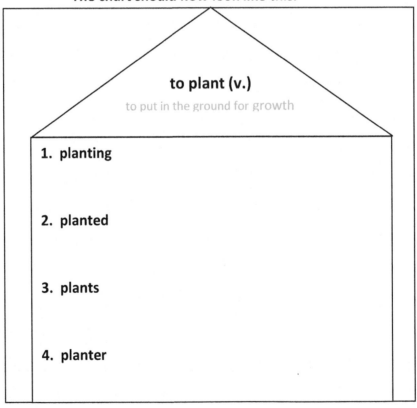

to plant (v.)
to put in the ground for growth

1. planting

2. planted

3. plants

4. planter

What if students don't know how to use the word in a sentence?

Morph House pushes students to use words that may sound familiar because they come from a known base word, but students are often unsure about how to actually use the less familiar word.

When this happens, go ahead and identify which part of speech students are going to use and direct them to the syntax rules.

Example: We are going to use "planter" as a noun. One syntax rule shows us that nouns can be subjects and that subjects go before verbs. We also know that articles, like "the" can go before nouns. So let's try using "The planter" as the subject to start our sentence. Make sure it is followed by a verb.

The planter holds rows of beautiful flowers.

Step 3- Students generate a sentence for each base word.

When first beginning this method, produce the sentences collaboratively. Consider the sample sentences from your lesson plan and steer students toward that type of sentence, thinking of both content and structure that you would like them to produce. They do not have to generate the exact sentence that you had planned, but you will have something to fall back on if they need guidance.

As students become more familiar with the method, they can complete their sentences in pairs, groups, or independently. If students are writing on the *Morph House* worksheet, they should only write the sentences *after* orally producing or repeating them as a class.

The chart should now look like this.

to plant (v.)

to put in the ground for growth

1. **planting**   The neighbors were planting new flowers while we were playing outside.

2. **planted**   In our science experiment, we studied two types of planted flowers.

3. **plants**   Some plants don't need much water to survive.

4. **planter**   Before the ceremony, new tulips were placed in the planter outside.

Step 4- Students identify parts of speech.

Show students the parts of speech clues triangle diagram and guide them through at least one sentence together, using all resources for clues (*Grammar Wall*, syntax rules, common endings table). Students are generally able to identify the suffix most easily. Help them decipher the word's function, or job, in the sentence and also its syntax, or position. Mark key features in the sentence to highlight the clues as you find them.

Continue to identify parts of speech collaboratively until students show ability to do so on their own. Once they can, students should complete this step in groups, pairs, or independently.

The chart should now look like this.

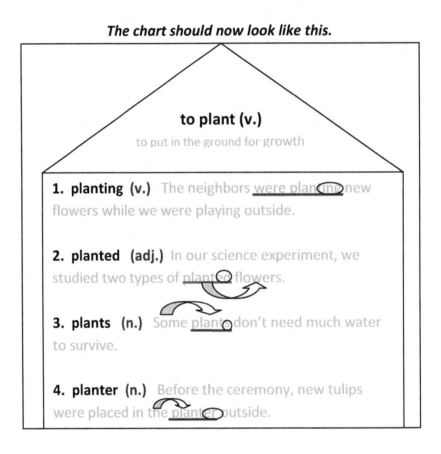

Step 5- Independent practice.

For independent practice, students can complete the worksheet for any remaining words on their own. If the entire worksheet was done collaboratively, ask students to write their own sentences for each of the derivatives. They can then switch sentences with a partner and identify the parts of speech.

Assessment

Student proficiency for correctly using derivatives can be assessed in the following ways:

- ✓ Students are given a base word and then must complete *Morph House* independently.
- ✓ Students are given sentences with derivatives and must identify the parts of speech.
- ✓ Students must fill in the blanks of a sentence with the most appropriate form of a base word.
- ✓ Students list derivatives of a base word.

What *Morph House* looks like across the language levels

Morph House can be completed with any language level. However, there are several components that will vary depending on student proficiency.

component/level	Beginner	Intermediate	Advanced
base word	basic vocabulary	academic vocabulary	academic vocabulary
number of derivatives	three-four	four-five	four or more
parts of speech to identify	noun, verb, adjective	noun, verb, adjective, adverb	noun, verb, adjective, adverb
other lesson components	-Can add affix chimney. -Whole lesson can be done collaboratively. -Can identify parts of speech based on function and suffix alone.	-can do half of the lesson collaboratively	-Last two-three words can be completed by students independently. -Identify parts of speech using all three criteria. -Write a second sentence for one of the derivatives, but using it as a different part of speech (*inspiring* as a verb or an adjective).

What this Method *Isn't*

It's <u>not</u> a long list of derivatives. Generating the derivatives for the base word comprises five minutes or less of the lesson. Students need guidance in correctly using these words in sentences.

It's <u>not</u> the time to invent words. As students learn affixes, they often overuse them resulting in new words, like *unplant*. Only actual words make it on the chart in *Morph House.* While affirming students' creativity, it's the teacher's responsibility to correct language errors and steer students toward language proficiency.

It's <u>not</u> a drawn-out vocabulary lesson. The teacher guides students in understanding the derivative based on the meaning of the base word and the affix. When more explanation is needed, the teacher acts as the living dictionary.

Things to Re-think

1. Could this method be a complete replacement for random lists of words students have to memorize?
2. Describe the school conditions under which most English learners have come to not know about how words are formed and that they can be congregated by families.
3. Compare this method with vocabulary development strategies associated with communicative approaches, i.e., *The Natural Approach, Total Physical Response (TPR),* and others. Which actually teaches vocabulary to students that they can use in academic sentences?
4. All the vocabulary learning in the world is useless if you can't form a correct sentence using the appropriate form of the word. Do you agree or disagree?

Administrators' Corner

<u>What to look for in *Morph House*</u>

➔ Is the method clearly labeled?

➔ Is there a chart prepared with the base word and definition at the top?

➔ Are the parts of speech clues posted for students to use?

➔ Does the chart show analysis to identify parts of speech?

➔ Are a variety of parts of speech used?

5. The most common reading intervention for poor secondary school readers is to teach them more vocabulary. Is this solid logic?
6. Academic vocabulary is viewed as Willy Wonka's Golden Ticket for English learners of all grade levels. How would you define the term *academic vocabulary*? Could it be defined as teaching morphological word families?

What to Expect

➤ "Why didn't they teach me this in elementary school?"

➤ " I have been trying to just memorize words until you taught us this?"

➤ "Hey!" "Those words actually go together!"

➤ "I never really understood the difference between *addition* and *adding* until you put those in the house."

➤ "A lot of the words you had us do in the house were on the state test, Mr. Scott."

Voices from the Classroom

Morph House has helped my students build their vocabulary, and have a deeper understanding of morphology and syntax. English Learners so often leave the –s or –ed off of a word, or don't see the connection between a noun form and adjective form of a word. This method has been a huge success in my classroom, and students are happy when they see a Morph House assignment. They know it will be challenging, but they feel confident after we've done it a few times. It ties in perfectly with the Grammar Wall, as they use that to try to build the word family.

—Adrianne from Moraga, CA

Grammar and Writing Methods

- *Verb Tense Study*

- *Syntax Surgery*

- *Four-Picture Story Frames*

What empirical research supports the explicit teaching of verb tenses to English learners?

Klein & Dittmar (1979) found that even the most basic morphology is often lacking from the speech of untutored immigrants. Krashen & Pon (1975) and Tarone (1985) showed a similar lack of morphological control even for classroom learners who could not monitor themselves effectively. Even after many years of exposure to the morphology of a second language, learners' morphological representations are shaky (DeKeyser, 2000; Johnson & Newport, 1989). The problem of L2 users' failure to demonstrate control over morphology structures is so fundamental it has spawned entire bodies of literature.

What empirical research supports the explicit teaching of syntax to English learners?

Linguists have been studying and researching syntax in humans, apes, and computers for quite a while. Here are some immediately relevant studies that provide grist for our New View of language teaching and learning, and the primordial role of syntax.

Mokhtari and Thompson (2006) analyzed fifth grade students' levels of syntactic awareness in relation to their reading fluency and reading comprehension. They found that the students' levels of syntactic awareness were significantly related to their reading fluency (r=.625) and reading comprehension performance (r=.816), indicating that lower levels of syntactic awareness corresponded to poor reading fluency and poor comprehension among this group of students. Other researchers have demonstrated the importance of syntax knowledge in the acquisition of reading by English learners (Catts et al., 1999; Siegel, 1993). The ability to understand the grammatical aspects of the language, according to this research, appears to be a critical factor for the fluent and efficient reading of text, largely due to the fact that fluent reading and efficient text reading requires predicting words that come next in a sequence.

Syntax deficits have been reported for poor readers learning to read in English (e.g., Gottardo, Stanovich, & Siegel, 1996; Siegel & Ryan, 1988; Tunmer & Hoover, 1992). Verhoeven (1994) suggested that English learners may have troubles learning to read in a second language because lexical and syntactic processing may not transfer from a first to a second language. Chiappe and Siegel (2006) used a cloze test to compare the syntactic competence of first-grade English learners and first-grade native English speakers. Native English speakers scored higher, a finding consistent with oral language difficulties revealed by other samples of ELL students (e.g., Geva, Yaghoub-Zadeh, & Schuster, 2000; Lesaux & Siegel, 2003; Swanson, Saez, Gerber, & Leafstedt, 2004). Syntactic awareness in the Chiappe and Siegel (2006) study of first grade EL students was an important predictor of the same students' second-grade reading achievement.

Verb Tense Conjugation

Old View

The learning and teaching of verb tenses took a big hit during the 1980s and beyond as acquisition views of language (what we are calling Old View 2.0) dominated teacher seminars, educational conferences, and teacher education programs. Looked at through the acquisition lens, verbs were described as too complex, too arbitrary, and too numerous to teach. As a result, the function of verbs in language was dismissed, and they were assigned no more importance than any other element of language that could be acquired by second language learners through the simple provision of *comprehensible input*.

The verb's role in comprehending text was further diminished as whole language literacy approaches became prevalent for teaching reading to English learners. Similarly, verbs and tenses—as objects of study-- were dismissed as irrelevant in writing, since the acquisition view focused mainly on "getting the gist" of what students were trying to communicate.

Simultaneously, new teachers received little to no formal instruction in the logic and structure of verb tenses, which fit nicely with an acquisition view of language that paid them little attention. Combined with many teachers' negative foreign

language experiences learning verb tenses, where poor methods of instruction were equated with verb tense learning as valueless, the stage was set for verbs to be banished.

New View

Paradoxically, the New View is really the Old View but with some important updates. Most of us who have studied a foreign language remember clearly—though not always fondly—the role verbs and tenses played in the curriculum of our foreign language courses. By the third semester, verb tenses usually comprised more than half of the content, and memorization and disciplined study were required to understand and use the logic of those tenses.

Like language teaching since the Greeks, the verb has historically assumed an altar of high importance, and for good reason. Quite simply, verbs are the axis upon which sentences turn. Verbs are the part of speech that allows us to express the range of thoughts and activities that permeate human life: moving, changing, having, knowing, helping, acting, intending, and causing (Pinker, 1994).

Without a knowledge and control of the verbs that express these concepts, sentences would be little more than word strings. Sentences, for all their glory, are built around verbs. Verbs are the chassis to which every other part of speech is attached. Put simply, verbs do a lot of the bossing around of the other parts of speech.

For second language learners, the concept of *verb*, its function, and its application must be taught if students are to have a solid foundation upon which to build more and more complex sentences.

 ## Reading Comprehension Connection

Read the following passage and try to determine its meaning:

The federal government on a crucial new role in the nation's health care, a basic benefits package for millions who not care.

By eliminating verbs in this short sentence, meaning is substantially impaired. Try this version, which provides the verbs, but in their un-conjugated forms.

The federal government to take on a crucial new role in the nation's health care, a basic benefits package for millions who to not have care.

While the content is made slightly clearer, we are still unsure of when any of these actions are happening. What if we randomly insert tenses—a popular practice among English learners lacking verb tense knowledge and instruction—to see if that helps.

The federal government to have taken on a crucial new role in the nation's health care, a basic benefits package for millions who are not going to have care.

Again, the random insertion of tenses does not help much. In fact, it can frequently make things worse. Because verbs play the role in sentences of specifying time and meaning, students who lack this knowledge consistently face roadblocks to reading comprehension. Not surprisingly, poor reading comprehension among English learners is frequently misdiagnosed as a global "comprehension" problem when more careful analysis of their language competence shows an underdeveloped or wholly absent understanding of what verbs communicate in sentences.

Academic Writing Connection

Jorge is a ninth-grade English learner who has just participated in a science experiment that involved mixing various chemicals together and testing the resulting substances. He understands the science as demonstrated by his ability to perform correctly the various experiments and his use of the measuring formula. When asked to write the results of his experiment, however, he is unable to use verbs in a way that captures what he did, what he learned, what he could have done, and what might have happened had he added different chemicals to the mix. In short, his writing is trapped by the three verb tenses he has been using predominantly for the past five years: simple past (-ed), present progressive (to be + verb + ing), and the simple future (will + verb). His essay, as a result, is not indicative of his learning and reads awkwardly.

> *I mixed different chemicals together. They reacted in different ways. The first chemical will change the other one. If I'm going to add the third chemical, something new is going to happen.*

He leaves the final question blank:

> *What would have happened if you had mixed the first chemical together with the third chemical first?*

Jorge is like thousands of English learners across the country. He has not been taught how verbs function and how to conjugate them in the tenses necessary for daily school work. Even his subject-verb agreement is frequently wrong, and his knowledge of tenses that appear in his textbooks is negligible. He understands their "gist" but cannot produce writing that sounds academic. He is left to apply and re-apply the few tenses he has managed to piece together over the past five years. Had he been instructed in verbs and their primacy in both the syntactic and semantic domains of reading comprehension, his essay may have sounded more like this.

> *By mixing the chemicals together, the result was (to be verb in the simple past) a mixture that reacted (simple past tense) differently when it was measured (simple past to be in the passive voice). The first chemical changed (simple past tense) the other one by neutralizing its acid content. If the first chemical had been mixed (past conditional) first with the third chemical, then the result would have been (future conditional) two different solutions that actually repel (simple present) each other.*

Students need *an understanding of verb tense meanings as well as control over their form and application to successfully participate in grade level academic content courses requiring reading or writing.*

Method

Verb Tense Study

Description

Students learn the form, meaning, and use of different verb tenses through direct teaching of a particular tense by the teacher. These lessons usually unfold over three to five days, and are presented through the use of teacher-made charts that clearly explain the tense, show how it is used, and explore how it serves to convey meaning.   The use of graphic organizers, different color text, and pictures help to support students as they work on mastering this important aspect of the English language.

Purpose

The purpose of this method is to teach how to conjugate verbs in different tenses and to use them in sentences that conform to certain verb tense formulas.

Materials Needed

- ☐ chart paper
- ☐ sentence strips
- ☐ different color markers
- ☐ color pictures measuring at least 5x7

Teacher Skills

- ✓ knowledge of verb tense form, meaning, and use
- ✓ knowledge of current student independent language level
- ✓ awareness of language level that students should be pushed to during the lesson
- ✓ knowledge of vocabulary and syntactic structures appropriate for targeted language level
- ✓ ability to form and manage students in pairs/groups to share answers
- ✓ question asking strategies to yield student answers in complete sentences
- ✓ question extension strategies to stretch student answers by using more complex grammatical structures
- ✓ ability to analyze sentences and lead students to do the same through focused questioning

Language Objective: We will produce _____ (number of sentences) complete sentences in the _____ (verb tense) _____ (declarative/negative/interrogative) form.

Steps

Before beginning a *Verb Tense Study,* students must be familiar with several prerequisite skills presented through "Concept Charts." On the following pages, you will see examples of the necessary charts. After the Concept Charts, we will look at the particular steps for the *Verb Tense Study* method. We will look at the "Steps at a Glance" followed by a more thorough discussion of each step along with examples.

Types of Sentences

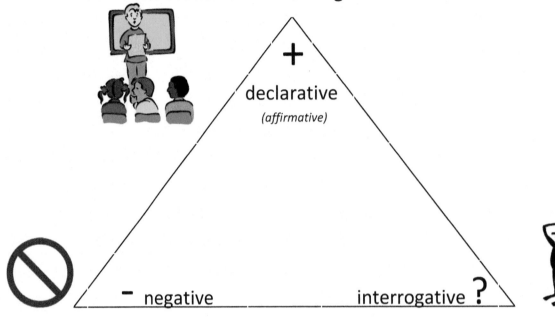

The students are learning verb tenses.

+

declarative

(affirmative)

− negative   interrogative ?

The students are **not**
learning verb tenses.

Are the students learning
verb tenses?

Type of sentence	Use	Punctuation	Example
Declarative	Telling sentence	.	The dog runs.
Negative (declarative)	"No" sentence	.	The dog does not run.
Interrogative	Asking sentence	?	Does the dog run?
Imperative	Command	.	Chase the dog please.
Exclamatory	Excitement	!	Wow! The dog runs fast!

Nouns

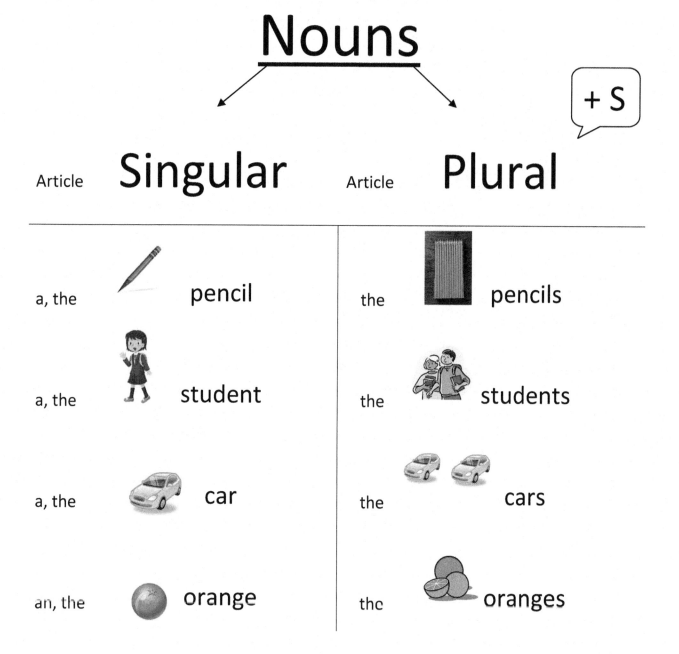

+ S

Article	Singular	Article	Plural
a, the	pencil	the	pencils
a, the	student	the	students
a, the	car	the	cars
an, the	orange	the	oranges

Verbs

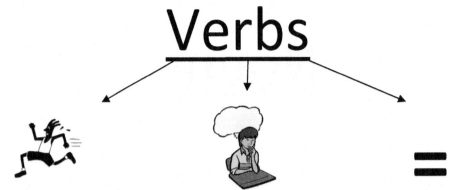

Physical Action   Mental Action   State of Being

Physical Action
- To jump
- To fly
- To sprint
- To land
- To blink
- To hover
- To catch_____
- To scrape_____
- To sprinkle_____
- To crush_____
- To lunge
- To growl
- To salute_____
- To ignite_____

Mental Action
- To think
- To acknowledge_____
- To accept_____
- To comprehend_____
- To evaluate_____
- To analyze_____
- To concentrate
- To compare_____
- To ponder_____
- To imagine_____
- To estimate_____
- To enjoy_____
- To discern_____
- To judge_____

State of Being

To be

am is are

was were

will be

being been

Other Linking Verbs
- To seem_____
- To appear_____
- To become_____
- To turn_____
- To grow_____
- To feel_____
- To sound_____
- To look_____

*Blanks after the verb ("to compare_____") signify that the verb is normally used as a transitive verb meaning that it requires an object (nous or pronouns) after it ("to compare ideas"). Conversely, intransitive verbs ("to growl") are fine without an object afterward.

Pronouns & To be Verbs

Personal Subject Pronoun		*Past*	*Present*	*Future*
Singular	**I**	was	am	will be
	you	were	are	will be
	he	was	is	will be
	she	was	is	will be
	it	was	is	will be
Plural	**we**	were	are	will be
	you	were	are	will be
	they	were	are	will be

Pronoun Pictures by Joel D. Castro

Verb Tense Study - Steps at a Glance

Preparation

1. Prepare Preview Chart
   (See examples on following pages.)
   a. Title
   b. Language Objective
   c. Parts of Speech
   d. Application (Why?)
   e. Formulas
   f. Example
2. Prepare Collaborative chart
   a. Select a picture that will yield sufficient subjects and verbs.
   b. Label headings for subject and verb.
   c. Pencil-in "push" words.
3. Design Independent Practice
   a. How many sentences will students write?
   b. What are the parameters for their sentences?
      i. number of words
      ii. types of subjects
      iii. types of verbs
      iv. interrogatives answered

Procedures

1. Teacher teaches the Preview Chart.
   a. Teacher asks questions for each part of the Preview Chart to increase student production and engagement.
2. Generate subjects and verbs
3. Sentence #1
   a. Teacher selects subject and verb to use.
   b. Teacher walks students through formula using prescribed subject and verb.
   c. Students finish sentence in pairs/groups.
   d. Teacher listens to three-four sentences from students.
   e. Teacher selects one sentence and stretches or extends.
   f. Students dictate sentence to teacher as he/she writes it
   **Analysis of sentence
4. Sentence #2
   a. Teacher selects subject and verb
   b. Students complete sentence in pairs/groups.
   c. Teacher listens to three-four sentences from students.
   d. Teacher selects one sentence and stretches or extends.
   e. Students dictate sentence to teacher as he/she writes it
   **Analysis of sentence
5. Sentence #3
   a. Students select subject and verb and create sentence in pairs/groups.
   b. Teacher listens to three-four sentences from students.
   c. Teacher selects one sentence and stretches or extends.
   d. Students dictate sentence to teacher as he/she writes it
   e. **Analysis of sentence
6. Independent Practice

Discussion of Steps

Before the lesson begins

* Go over Concept Charts before beginning the first *Verb Tense Study*

Step 1-Create the Preview Chart

Each *Verb Tense Study* lesson is directed by a Preview Chart made by the teacher. The Preview Chart serves as a guide and resource for the entire lesson. After the lesson, students can refer to it when applying the same verb tense in their writing. For this reason, the chart should be clear, easy to read, and neat. Use a consistent format for each chart with colors that can be easily read and sentence strips for the formula as they will direct sentence construction.

Each Preview Chart has five essential components that must be on every chart.

They are:

1. **Language Objective:** The language objective clearly states what students will produce during the lesson including sentence form (declarative, negative, interrogative), verb tense, and any other key grammatical features.
2. **Parts of Speech:** This section is meant to outline the types of verbs students will utilize as well as any rules dictating form. For example, using a singular subject versus a plural subject often requires a different form of the verb (was/were). Students should be able to refer to this section of the Preview Chart for a clear and ready explanation of which verb to use and when.
3. **Application (Why?):** The application section of the chart indicates the reason one would use the specified tense as well as the meaning. The formula and parts of speech section explain the "how" whereas the application answers "why."
4. **Formulas:** For each form of sentence that will be practiced, students need to see a corresponding formula. Thus, if students will learn declarative (affirmative), negative and interrogative forms, three formulas are needed. The formula should be written on a sentence strip not only for emphasis, but also for use in other methods. The key components of the formula (subject and verb) should be clearly highlighted to alert students to their importance in the sentence.
5. **Examples:** Under each formula an example sentence that follows the formula is written. The example sentence should have the same key components highlighted as the formula.

An example of a completed Preview Chart and a blank template can be found on the following pages. The blank template can be used to draft any *Verb Tense Study* Preview Chart. For complete Preview Charts for each verb tense, please refer to *The Painless, Plan-less Grammar Guide.*

(Title)

Language Objective:	Parts of Speech:

Application (Why?):

Formulas & Examples
(Formula 1)
(Example 1)
(Formula 2)
(Example 2)
(Formula 3)
(Example 3)

Present Perfect

Language Objective: We will write complete sentences in the Present Perfect verb tense in three forms: -declarative, -negative, -interrogative.	**Parts of Speech:** *Verbs* **has/have + past participle** singular subject- **has** plural subject- **have** (I/you)

Application (Why?):

We use the Present Perfect to show actions that:

- have recently ended,
- started in the past but may continue in the present,
- happened in the past but the time is unknown or unimportant (relate an experience).

Formulas & Examples

Declarative

Subject + has/have + past participle + finisher.

(Example 1)

The neighboring countries have battled over the disputed territory for centuries.

Negative

Subject + has/have + not + past participle + finisher.

(Example 2)

The President has not spoken to the public since last month.

Interrogative

Has/Have + subject + past participle + finisher?

(Example 3)

Have rescuers found the missing divers yet?

Step 2- Create the Collaborative Chart

Verb Tense Studies are generally taught over multiple days. The first day focuses on the declarative form with subsequent days focusing on the negative and interrogative forms. When one formula is introduced per day, one Collaborative Chart is also presented per day. Unlike the Preview Chart, which is completed before the lesson begins, the Collaborative Chart is completed with students during the lesson. However, certain aspects of the Collaborative Chart need to be prepared prior to the lesson:

1. **Subject/Verb headings:** Label singular and plural subjects if both are to be used. Leave space for four-six subjects/verbs.

2. **Picture:** The teacher selects a picture to use on the Collaborative Chart before the lesson begins. The picture can be content related so long as students are *already* familiar with the content. (This is not the place to introduce a new content-related concept.) In looking at the picture, students should be able to readily generate a few subjects and verbs.

3. **"Push" words:** In order to advance students to the next language level, they will need to use higher level vocabulary and syntactic structures. To prepare for this "push," teachers can pencil-in desired subjects and verbs directly on the Collaborative Chart or write them on a separate note. Teachers can also plan to "outlaw" or prohibit the use of certain, overly-used subjects and/or verbs (e.g. man, kid, to play).

Tip!

For the subject of the picture, lead students away from using inanimate nouns (e.g. mountain, grass, chair). While they may be present in the picture, it will be difficult to attribute actions to them.

Step 3- Design Independent Practice

It's important to know where and how you want the lesson to end before it has even started. With the goal in mind, planning for the lesson becomes more focused. The end goal for the *Verb Tense Study* is the independent practice, which can be done at the end of the lesson or as homework. Teachers should consider the parameters for the independent practice. Specifically, the following questions must be answered:

- How many sentences will students be expected to write independently?
- Is there a word-minimum for student sentences? What is it?
- What types of subjects and verbs will students be allowed to use?
- What details should students include in the finisher (where, why, when, etc.)?
- Where will students write their sentences: a language journal, a loose sheet of paper?
- Will students be responsible for analyzing their sentences in the same way as done on the Collaborative Chart?

During the Lesson

Step 1- Present the Preview Chart

Each *Verb Tense Study* lesson begins here. The teacher introduces the chart and engages students in the presentation. To keep this part of the lesson from sounding like a lecture, try stopping after each of the five key parts of the Preview Chart and engaging students by either having them read with you or by asking them a comprehension question (Examples for Parts of Speech: "Which two types of verbs will we need today?" and "Which 'to be' verb will we use with a plural subject?").

Step 2- Generate subjects and verbs

Generate four to six subjects and four to six verbs. Remember to include both singular and plural subjects if both will be used during the lesson. Remember to write all verbs in the infinitive form ("to run"= infinitive, run or runs= conjugated verb) so that students consciously go through the work of conjugating the verb into the desired verb tense.

This part of the lesson is meant to take no more than ten minutes for the subjects and verbs together (five minutes for each). However, make sure that students are lead to use the "push" words that have been prepared.

Step 3- Collaborative Sentence #1

The first collaborative sentence on the Collaborative Chart is meant to be explicitly guided by the teacher so that students *only* use the prescribed formula. To that end, the teacher selects the subject and verb for students

> **Tip!**
>
> *Three ways to include "push" words*
>
> 1. When students provide an overly used word (boy), **ask a question that leads to a more specific term.** Example: "Yes, it is a boy, but what's the name of someone who plays on a baseball team and throws the ball to the batter?" (Pitcher.) In this case, "boy" does not need to be written down in favor of writing only the "push" word.
>
> 2. **Provide a higher level synonym** for a known word. Example: Write down "to hold" under verbs and draw an arrow to "to grasp." Explain to students the difference and have them act it out.
>
> 3. Rather than playing an extended guessing game, charades, or "sounds like" just **teach students a new word** that you want them to use and explain what it means. For higher level students, consider choosing a word that might be in their lexicon but for which they don't have semantic control. Ask them, "How does the verb, __("push" word) apply to this picture?"

to use in the sentence. Because the teacher will be guiding this sentence, it's a perfect time to use some of the "push" words generated during the brainstorming. Once the subject and verb are selected, the teacher walks back to the formula and students read the formula but now substitute in the selected subject and verb. As students approach the verb part of the formula, the teacher stops to ask students what form the verb will be in and why. Students should be able to answer this question from their review of the Preview Chart.

> ### Tip!
> All students must be able to orally produce the sentence before the teacher can write it. It may take more than one oral practice or partner-share before all students have the sentence.

With the base of the sentence (subject + verb) read by the whole class, the teacher then instructs the students to finish the sentence by answering specific questions ("Complete this sentence by telling me 'when,' 'where,' 'why,' or 'how' it happened."). Students complete their sentences in pairs or groups. The teacher then calls on three to four students to share their sentences. The teacher selects one sentence or aspects of more than one and now asks students to dictate the sentence so that he/she can write it. Students can now write the sentence as well.

When the sentence is written on the Collaborative Chart, the teacher then asks analysis questions for the sentence. The analysis questions cannot be overlooked as they are what link the sentence to the Preview Chart and specifically the objective of the lesson. Students should be able to find the answers to the analysis questions on the Preview Chart or other language resources in the room. By the end of the analysis, the collaborative sentence should be marked in so that the language objective is clearly identifiable.

Examples of Analysis Questions

- What is the subject of the sentence?
- What is/are the verb(s) in the sentence?
- How did we conjugate the verb?
- Why did we conjugate the verb as we did? ("Why did we add an *s* to the verb?")
- How can you tell the sentence is written in the _____ tense?
- What verb tense is the sentence written in and how do you know?
- Why did we use the _____ verb tense? (Refer students to the Application section of the Preview Chart.)

Step 4- Collaborative Sentence #2

For the second sentence on the Collaborative Chart, the procedures are similar to that of the first but the teacher does less guiding. The teacher still selects the subject and the verb for students to use but then allows students to complete their sentences on their own and in accordance with the formula. Again, the teacher listens to a few student-produced sentences and then selects one or aspects of more than one for the whole class to produce together.

The second sentence presents an opportune time for teachers to extend or otherwise stretch a sentence. For example, if students produce the sentence, "The classmates were observing the butterflies during science class last Tuesday." the teacher can ask students to move the "when" of the sentence ("during science class last Tuesday") to the beginning of the sentence yielding, "During science class last Tuesday, the classmates were observing the butterflies." This extension pushes students to practice an unfamiliar syntactic structure in which the subject is not the first part of the sentence.

> *Tip!*
> Count the number of words per collaborative sentence. Set the average number of words as the minimum of words allowed in students' independent sentences.

After all students have orally produced the sentence, the teacher writes the sentence as students dictate it. Students are then asked analysis questions about the sentence and the sentence is marked to indicate tense and other features.

Step 5- Collaborative Sentence #3

As the teacher continues to give more responsibility for the sentence creation to the students, the students now select their own subject and verb and create a sentence in their pairs/groups. The teacher then listens to a variety of sentences and once again selects a sentence for students to extend with guidance. Students dictate the sentence to the teacher as he/she writes it and the collaborative section ends with sentence analysis and marking for the objective.

> *Tip!*
> *Five easy ways to extend sentences*
> 1. Ask students to answer a specific interrogative. ("Tell me 'where' or 'why.'")
>
> 2. Ask students to move certain elements (the "where" or "when") to different part s of the sentence.
>
> 3. Ask students to include an adjective to describe a particular noun in the sentence.
>
> 4. Combine ideas from more than one sentence so that students have to use more than one subject, verb, or even clause.
>
> 5. Use another "push" word somewhere else in the sentence.

<u>Step 6- Independent Practice</u>

The teacher directs students to complete a set number of sentences independently that follow the formula. Students can be instructed to use only the subjects and verbs from the Collaborative Chart or can be allowed to use others. Since students must follow the formula, the teacher can instruct students to copy the formula before they begin writing. Independent work can easily be finished as homework or assigned as homework.

Assessment

Student proficiency for the prescribed verb tense can be assessed in many ways. Below are a few examples.

- ✓ Grade students' written independent work. Check that sentences follow the formula and that the subject and verb agree. Students can also be graded on correctly identifying the subject and the verb of the sentence.
- ✓ Present only a formula to students and ask them to complete a given number of sentences that follow that formula.
- ✓ Provide students with a subject and verb and ask them to complete a sentence in a given verb tense.
- ✓ Pass out pictures to individuals or groups of students. Students then complete their own "mini" *Verb Tense Study* by generating subjects and verbs and then creating sentences.
- ✓ Provide a completed sentence in one tense and ask students to re-write it another tense.
- ✓ Provide a completed sentence in one form (negative) and ask students to re-write it in a different form (declarative).
- ✓ After studying a verb tense, ask students to create their own Preview Chart and present it to the class.

What the *Verb Tense Study* looks like across the language levels

The *Verb Tense Study* is a method that can be completed with any language level. The main differentiation among the language levels would be the actual verb tense instructed. For example, beginning students would need to match subject pronouns to "to be" verbs in the present, while the same task would be too simple for advanced and even intermediate students, who could benefit more from explicit instruction on modals and the conditional tenses. Teachers can consult their district or school's grammar timeline or scope and sequence to find out which tenses are most appropriate for their students. Likewise, *The Painless, Plan-Less Grammar Guide* (Lightning Source Publishing) divides verb tenses into basic and advanced levels while providing a general order to follow.

Though all language levels can benefit from the *Verb Tense Study* method, there should be some differences between charts from classes of different levels. Use the chart below for some basic guidelines.

chart feature/level	**Beginner**	**Intermediate**	**Advanced**
types of subjects	-subject pronouns -common nouns -proper nouns	-compound subjects -content-related subjects - collective nouns	-appositives -content-related subjects -subjects with adjective clauses (The custodian who works at night...)
types of verbs	-physical action -common verbs -intransitive verbs	-transitive verbs -content-related physical action -mental action -phrasal verbs	-transitive verbs -intransitive verbs -content-related physical action -mental action -phrasal verbs -linking verbs -modals
length of collaborative sentences	5-10 words	10-15 words	15+ words
parts of speech that start each sentence	-nouns -pronouns -articles	-no subject pronouns -adjectives -prepositions -adverbs	-adverbs -prepositions -conjunctions -gerunds
number of elements (who, what, where, when, why, how) addressed in each sentence	-formula + one/two -where or when	-formula + two-four -where, when, why, how	-formula + four or more -multiples of different elements

What this Method *Isn't*

It's <u>not</u> a vocabulary guessing game. Provide the desired "push" word to students if they don't know it.

It's <u>not</u> a vocabulary list. Limit the generation of subjects and verbs to ten minutes. The goal is the creation of sentences in the specified verb tense, not a list of words.

It's <u>not</u> an exercise in which students practice familiar and comfortable sentences. Every sentence that is written on the Collaborative Chart should be reflective of a new syntactic feature that students are learning. If they can already produce the sentence independently, there's no point in going through the steps of the lesson.

It's <u>not</u> a competition to see who can write the longest sentence by endlessly adding "and" or 13 adjectives in front of the subject. Challenging students to lengthen their sentences should be focused and within guided parameters. Tell students they're allowed one "and" per sentence and lead them to use the less familiar parts of speech.

Things to Re-think

1. How have your own experiences with foreign-language verb learning affected your views of teaching verbs to English learners?

2. What evidence can educators produce to support the parochial view that English learners will "acquire" verb tense mastery through "exposure" to the English language?

3. What do your experiences of reading the academic writing of English learners tell you

---

Administrators' Corner

<u>What to look for in a *Verb Tense Study*</u>

➔ Is the method clearly labeled?

➔ Is there a Preview Chart prepared and in place before the lesson begins?

➔ Can all students easily read and access the Preview Chart from where they are seated?

➔ Are the formulas written on sentence strips?

➔ Are the sentences marked to clearly identify the language objective?

➔ Is the Collaborative chart prepared for the lesson?

➔ Has an appropriate picture been chosen?

➔ Are previous Collaborative charts posted somewhere?

➔ Compare the sentences from previous Collaborative charts to the sentences on the current Collaborative chart. Has there been any progress?

➔ Check number of words/sentence.

➔ Check the subjects and verbs.

➔ Do classrooms of different language levels show different levels of student production?

➔ Use the following "Procedural Observation Sheet" to help teachers follow the steps of the *Verb Tense Study*.

about their verb tense knowledge and control?

4. How can English learners have high levels of reading comprehension if they don't know and understand how verbs and tenses function?

5. Could teaching verb tenses to English learners be considered a sensible and high-return "reading intervention"?

What to Expect

➢ As the old adage goes, if your only tool is a hammer, then all of your problems are viewed as nails. And so it goes with many English learners who are certain that their habitual ways of using a finite number of verb tenses can solve any time, tense or mood need. *I take lots of pictures two weeks ago* is one example of how students strategically work around not knowing.

➢ The idea that verb tenses conform to certain inviolable formulas is likely to be a new dawn for many of your students. Some will thank you for engineering this epiphany, while others will demand to know how and why this secret has been kept from them for so long. A few might quietly ask if you would allow them to write all of the formulas in their notebooks so they can begin practicing.

➢ Managing the steps in this method can initially take some practice. Like learning a new dance, an unfamiliar computer program or wearing new shoes, you may feel unsure about the totality of the method or stumble over some of the steps. But here is the good news: your students are learning the method along with you, so look at it as a team project.

➢ Students will resort to their tried-and-true practice of simplifying things. They will identify simple subjects from the picture (boy, lady, student, do) and try to run uber-simple (read: comfortable and well-rehearsed) verbs up the flag pole (to like, to run, to smile). Have your fly swatter ready to crush these hackneyed and somewhat Pavlovian responses. The output of this method is only as good as its input.

➢ Your repeated requests for students to justify their knowledge (*How do you know the verb is in the past perfect tense?*) may not win you favorite teacher of the week in the early going of this method. But this is the "beef" of the method in many ways, so stay with it. They will come to see that you are actually helping them, even though it hurts.

Voices from the Classroom

The Verb Tense Study method has allowed me to teach grammar in an accessible and equitable manner. Students clearly understand the task at hand as the verb tense is presented in a formulaic yet engaging way. The three forms, in conjunction with the Grammar Wall, have helped my students' writing as the now know how to appropriately use verb tenses in writing. It has also made their writing clearer as they are now adding more details. Overall, the Verb Tense Study method has made grammar engaging and fun. I now have students competing to see who can write the most detailed, yet grammatically correct sentence!

–Ivette from Fremont, CA

The Verb Tense Study method has helped me connect other content areas to my students' language development. They are no longer sitting in the back of a room not participating because lack of language with regards to the content area. Due to this method as well as many others, I am constantly making sure that my students are talking, discovering new words and pushing them to the next level. I had a beginning student tell me "thank you" because I helped him participate in his science class. He was able to use the vocabulary we had developed using the Verb Tense Study in his class in order to help his group understand a concept. The smile on his face is what constantly encourages me to continue to push my students and make connections with other curriculum. I think many people get stuck in developing basic language skills without pushing their students beyond so that they can access and use academic language which is essential to their success.

–Rebekah from Dixon

Preview Chart
☐ Language objective
☐ Parts of speech
☐ Student response?
☐ Application
☐ Student demonstration of understanding?
☐ Formula
☐ Example
☐ Analysis by students?

Brainstorming
☐ Show picture.
☐ Generate subjects in complete sentences? Number of subjects: _____
☐ Generate verbs in complete sentences? Number of verbs:_____

Collaborative Sentence #1
☐ Teacher selects subject and verb.
☐ Teacher points to formula for *students* to generate sentence.
☐ Students pair-share to complete sentence.
☐ Teacher extends sentence with interrogatives.
☐ Students *orally* complete sentence before teacher writes.
☐ Teacher writes sentence as students say it.
☐ Analysis of sentence.

Analysis Questions:

_____

_____

Collaborative Sentence #2
☐ Teacher selects subject and verb.
☐ Students pair-share to complete sentence.
☐ Teacher extends sentence with interrogatives.
☐ Students *orally* complete sentence before teacher writes.
☐ Teacher writes sentence as students say it.
☐ Analysis of sentence.

Analysis Questions:

_____

_____

Collaborative Sentence #3
☐ Students pair-share to complete sentence.
☐ Teachers extend with interrogatives.
☐ Students *orally* complete sentence before teacher writes it.
☐ Teacher writes sentence as students say it.
☐ Analysis of sentence.

Analysis Questions:

_____

_____

Independent Sentences
☐ Guidelines for writing

Guidelines: _____

Syntax

Old View

For about the past 30 years, most teachers have heard in their teacher preparation courses and during in-services that students naturally "acquire" language. This simplistic aphorism logically resulted in the almost total abandonment of grammar teaching for English learners, native English speakers, and even teachers! The results have been devastating, especially for English learners: they pick up a few basic sentence structures that they use over and over again in ways that frequently reflect incorrect sentence structure. Educators, for their part, lament the poor grammar but keep holding out that students will eventually "acquire" all of the sentence grammar necessary to complete a 22-word sentence that correctly communicates their analysis of how an author could have altered the plot structure by utilizing additional metaphors. Instead, the thousands of students from the "osmosis" theory of learning sentence structure write: *The character is a good man and he helps the lady.*

The Old View 2.0 has no way to explain sentence structure, or the ordering of words. Its key components are:

- Grammar is too difficult to teach and is full of just too many rules, so don't bother teaching it.

- Students will learn English grammar by listening to people use sentences.

- Teachers must provide something called "comprehensible input" (Krashen, 1984) so that students can acquire all the English sentences they will need.

- Students must be comfortable and experience no stress during this process.

- Reading books in English will help them to learn more sentences and more about sentence structure.

- Writing development is "last" in the hierarchical development of language, so find alternative assessments until they can write. Dioramas can be a nifty way to demonstrate one's understanding of the key human themes and concepts in *The Crucible*.

New View

Language is comprised of many different parts that are used together to communicate with others. These parts of language go together according to fixed rules. English is no different. Proficient English speakers have a wide array of sentences they can form, sometimes without overtly knowing what rules they are applying. For someone learning a new language, however, trying to "figure out" sentence structure in the absence of direct teaching about the structure often results in frustration and fossilized low language competence.

By looking at language taxonomically, certain rules and patterns become evident that are used again and again. Much like music composers rely on scales to create melodies and chords, English learners need to know which "notes" are available and how to combine them to "make music." The New View states the obvious: students learn English best and faster when they are taught how words are put together to make sentences. Aspects of this approach are:

- The parts of language can be identified and taught based on their function in a sentence.

- There *are* rules for putting the words in the correct order that are learnable and useful.

- We can index the rules from simple to complex.

- Mastery of simple sentence structure concepts creates the foundation for mastering more complex skills.

- Certain language structures are necessary—especially in school settings—to convey certain ways of thinking.

- Comprehension flows through the sentence structures we understand. More structures yield more comprehension. Fractured structures or absent structures thwart comprehension.

Reading Comprehension Connection

Books—whether they be science texts, literature anthologies, or economics tomes—are full of sentences that follow prescribed grammar rules. Most of us would have little patience trying to read a book that featured sentences with consistently fractured grammatical constructions. As we read, we gain meaning from the text, though we give little thought to the structure of the sentences that we are reading. But our comprehension can also be viewed as a sentence structure undertaking. We are able to comprehend a text because the words are ordered in ways that allow meaning to flow from the beginning to the end of the sentence. Moreover, the sentence structures that we are reading are also sentence structures that we can use to produce similar sentences. Put simply, the words and the order rules that constrain their positions serve as the tracks along which our comprehension rolls, just like a train shuttles along a connected series of ties and track to its destination.

On a daily basis English learners confront a multitude of sentences in books for which the structure of the sentences is completely foreign to them. Sadly, their lack of knowledge about sentence structure does not allow them to analyze the sentence to gain meaning. Instead— and we have all seen this behavior—they look for the few words they know and then make a guess as to what the sentence could be about. In the worst case, they say the words, hoping against hope that by hearing them meaning will somehow arrive. This binary approach to understanding text—I either know what this means or I don't—can hardly be characterized as either strategic or effective. But to the non-grammar instructed English learner, what other choice do they have?

 ## Academic Writing Connection

To write about complex ideas and concepts, students need to be able to use complex language structures and sentences. For example, read the following sentence:

If one of the other non-essential chemicals had been added to the mixture, it could be safely assumed that the result might be different than what was previously forecast.

Wow, that is a mouthful. But it says exactly what needs to be said with respect to the science experiment it describes. By contrast, an English learner who is bereft of sentence structure formation is left to write something that sounds like this: *The experiment has lots of problems.* As we have mentioned throughout this book, the link between school tasks and grammar is one that is frequently not addressed in teacher education programs. Let's dig a little deeper into this provocative concept.

Most school learning tasks are disguised language tasks. If students are not taught the language rules and structures necessary for doing those tasks, e.g. describe, analyze, compare, differentiate, decide, then they are left without the tools and knowledge that are frequently assumed by teachers. For example, if we want students to be able to describe the similarities or differences between two things or people, they would need to be able to use, among other language skills, a verb construction (is/are, for example), a comparative adjective (bigger, taller, faster) that is then followed by the word *than* (adverb), and then juxtaposed against the first item. *Geese fly faster than many smaller birds on their way to food sources.* What if we wanted our students to understand and write about a possible action other than what actually occurred? This sort of hypothesizing is a common academic writing task. *If the main character had known that her friend lied, she would not have told her such private information.* By looking at the sentence's various parts grammatically, we can see that such a sentence—easy for us—uses grammatical items to reflect a way of thinking, i.e., assuming a contrary condition and then advancing an alternative and hypothetical course of action. To repeat, complex grammar concepts underlie and are necessary for complex academic writing. We must make those underlying grammar skills the focus of our ELD instruction.

Students need to apply common syntax rules to the construction and comprehension of sentences.

Method

Syntax Surgery

Description

Students correctly form a sentence from mixed-up words based by using syntax rules.

Purpose

By re-assembling mixed-up sentences, students can slow down the syntax of English and visually see how words are ordered. Students apply newly learned syntax rules to accurately construct sentences in the English language.

Materials Needed

- ☐ one sentence cut into pieces word by word (sentence strips or index cards)
- ☐ sets of words on pieces of paper for student use (if using "Hands-on" approach)
- ☐ class set of syntax rules
- ☐ *Grammar Wall*

Teacher Skills

- ✓ knowledge of English syntax rules
- ✓ ability to explain and apply syntax rules with English language learners
- ✓ knowledge of current student independent language level
- ✓ awareness of language level that students should be pushed to during the lesson
- ✓ knowledge of vocabulary and syntactic structures appropriate for language level
- ✓ ability to form and manage students in pairs/groups to share answers
- ✓ question asking strategies to yield student answers in complete sentences

Steps

While *Syntax Surgery* can be done independently of other methods, it can also be used to practice previously learned verb tenses and structures used in *Verb Tense Study*. The *Syntax Surgery* method can be instructed in two ways, either "Hands-on," in which students physically manipulate the words of the sentence or through "Eyes-on," in which students only see the teacher's set of words before reconstructing the sentence in written form on a piece of paper. Both approaches follow the same steps for lesson instruction. These steps will be looked at on the next page in an overview and are thereafter more fully discussed.

Language Objective: We will assemble a complete sentence based on our knowledge of syntax and the eight parts of speech.

Syntax Surgery - Steps at a Glance

Preparation

1. Prepare lesson plan.
    a. What are the key grammatical features that students will need to use?
    b. What are the syntax rules that will be needed?
    c. Which verb tense will be used?
        i. Is the Preview Chart for that tense posted?
    d. Write out the guided reconstruction steps.
    e. When will students receive their own words ("Hands-on") or be allowed to start writing the sentence ("Eyes-on")?
    f. Write out at least five shuffles.
2. Write out sentence on sentence strip or index cards for teacher use.
    a. Write extra words for shuffles.
3. Create words for students to use (for "Hands-on" approach).
    a. Leave blanks for shuffles.

Procedures

Teacher reveals mixed-up sentence as students read words.

Guided Reconstruction

1. Find the possible verbs in the sentence.
2. Find the possible subjects in the sentence.
3. Match the possible subjects and verbs to form clauses.
4. Find the possible adjectives.
5. Match the adjectives to the nouns or pronouns.
6. Find the pronouns.
7. Place pronouns after referring to the noun it replaces.
8. Find the possible prepositions.
9. Match the prepositions to nouns.
10. Find the conjunctions.
11. Match the conjunctions to clauses, words, or groups of words.
12. Find the possible adverbs.
13. Match the adverbs to verbs, adjectives or adverbs.

Shuffles

- Shorten the sentence to the main clause.
- Change the form of the sentence from declarative to negative.
- Change the form of the sentence to the interrogative form.
- Change the subject of the sentence from singular to plural or plural to singular.
- Move one phrase or clause to another part of the sentence.
- Change the tense of the sentence.
- Replace key words with synonyms.
- Replace key words with a different word from the same part of speech.
- Add a new feature to the sentence.

Grammar Wall

Students post words from the sentence on the Grammar Wall by identifying the appropriate part of speech and justifying their answers.

Syntax Surgery Lesson Plan

Original Sentence:	Verb Tense:
	Other Key Grammatical Features:

Language Objective:

Guided reconstruction steps:

1.

2.

3.

4.

5.

Shuffles *(That address verb tense and grammatical features.)*	New Sentence
Shuffle 1:	
Shuffle 2:	
Shuffle 3:	
Shuffle 4:	
Shuffle 5:	

Possible shuffles:

Discussion of Steps

Before the lesson begins

<u>Step 1-Prepare the Lesson Plan</u>

Syntax is a component of language that we don't often discuss as teachers. As such, it is very difficult to reconstruct a mixed-up sentence without relying on, "It sounds right." In order to be prepared to lead students through a syntax-based exercise, you must understand the syntax rules yourself and have a plan for guiding students through them.

We will now go over the lesson template form found on the previous page:

1. **Original Sentence:** In this box, write the sentence that students will reconstruct.
2. **Verb Tense/Other Key Grammatical Features:** The verb tense will be a main clue in reconstructing the sentence so make sure that students are familiar with the verb tense that is used and have resources (Preview Chart) available for reference. Likewise, you can also highlight any other key grammatical features (compound subject, adverb of frequency, subordinating conjunction, etc.) that you would like students to focus on based on previous learning. Any key verb tenses or grammatical features can be manipulated during the "shuffles" portion of the lesson.
3. **Language Objective:** The objective of the lesson will always be to reconstruct a sentence based on English syntax rules. However, the particular foci of the lesson (verb tense, grammatical features) can change.

> **Tip!**
> *Selecting a sentence for Syntax Surgery*
> * Use a recently studied verb tense.
> * Use grammatical features previously studied.
> * Consider using a topic from another content area.
> * Look at the average number of words in students' independent writing and use a few more for the guided sentence.
> * Limit the number of new vocabulary words to two.
> * Limit the number of syntax rules that will be used to two new rules for every sentence.
> * Use a sentence directly from a grade-level content-area textbook.

Guided Reconstruction Steps:

Probably the most challenging portion of the lesson to prepare is the process students will need to go through to correctly order the sentence without relying on, "It sounds right." On the next page, you'll find a table of the basic syntax rules, followed by a discussion of which rules to introduce and when. If teaching syntax for the first time, this set of rules will be sufficient for use by the class. Only guide students through the syntax rules that apply to the sentence.

Basic Syntax Rules

1.	Subject + verb. noun pronoun	He walks.
2.	adjective + noun	The red ball
3.	= noun + linking verb + adjective (or pronoun) (linking verb= am, is, are, etc.)	The ball is red.
4.	noun ⟺ pronoun	(Pronoun replaces noun after noun is introduced.)
5.	preposition + noun (= prepositional phrase)	under the bridge
6.	OR adverb + verb + adverb	quietly reads **or** reads quietly
7.	Clause + conjunction + clause. (subject + verb) (subject + verb)	The students must stay inside because it is raining.
8.	Conjunction + clause, clause. (subordinating) (subject + verb) (subject + verb)	Because it is raining, the students must stay inside.
9.	verb + noun (transitive verb) (direct object)	Throw the ball.
10.	= noun + linking verb + noun (or pronoun) (to be verbs, to seem, etc.)	Whales are mammals.
11.	Noun + linking verb + prepositional phrase. (or pronoun) (to be verbs, to seem, etc.)	Squirrels were in the tree.
12.	_____ + coordinating conjunction + _____ (Can join **nouns, pronouns, verbs, prepositions, adjectives, adverbs**)	chocolate or vanilla

Still want to know where to start with the Guided Reconstruction? While there are more than the 12 basic syntax rules supplied on the prior page, these basic steps will allow your class to reconstruct even content-area text at the secondary level. However, not all of the rules apply all of the time. Look at the table below to help you decide the order in which you should use the syntax rules in guided reconstruction.

Syntax Rule Frequency	
Most Sentences	**Less Frequent**
<ul><li>**subject + verb**</li><li>**adjective + noun**</li><li>**preposition + noun**</li></ul>	<ul><li>noun + linking verb + adjective</li><li>noun-pronoun</li><li>adverb + verb/ verb + adverb</li><li>clause + conjunction + clause/ conjunction + clause, + clause</li><li>noun + linking verb + noun</li><li>noun + linking verb + prepositional phrase</li><li>____ + coordinating conjunction + ____</li></ul>

Shuffles

Prepare at least five shuffles for each lesson. Shuffles should focus on the verb tense and key grammatical features that the teacher has highlighted for the lesson. Consult the table of possible shuffles below. We recommend that the first three shuffles be practiced in every lesson.

Sentence: *Olympic athletes have been training at this arena for the past three months.*

Shuffle	Resulting Sentence (Resulting changes are underlined.)
Shorten the sentence to the main clause (subject + verb)	Olympic athletes have been training.
Change the form of the sentence from declarative to negative.	Olympic athletes have not been training.
Change the form of the sentence from declarative to interrogative.	Have Olympic athletes been training?
Put original sentence back together.	Olympic athletes have been training at this arena for the past three months.
Change the subject from plural to singular.	The Olympic athlete has been training at this arena for the past three months.
Move the "when" phrase (prepositional phrase of time) to another part of the sentence.	For the past three months, Olympic athletes have been training at this arena.
Change the tense of the sentence. (present perfect progressive to present perfect)	Olympic athletes have trained at this arena for the past three months.
Replace a key word with a synonym.	Olympic athletes have been practicing at this arena for the past three months.
Replace a key word with a word from the same part of speech. (preposition)	Olympic athletes have been training near this arena for the past three months.
Add a new feature. (adverb of frequency)	Olympic athletes have been training daily at this arena for the past three months.

Step 2- Write out Sentence for Teacher Use

This is the sentence that students will look at during guided reconstruction so it should be easy to read for all students. We suggest writing it on sentence strips or index cards.

Step 3- Create Words for Student Use ("Hands-on")

Teachers can write or type the words (out of order) on a template such as the one provided. Students can either cut the words themselves or teachers can pre-cut them to save instructional time.

*On the following pages, you'll find and example lesson plan as well as the student words that accompany it.

Syntax Surgery Lesson Plan

Original Sentence: On the court, the coach is observing the athletes while they practice.	Verb Tense: Present Progressive
	Other Key Grammatical Features: subordinating conjunction of time, preposition of location

Language Objective: We will arrange the sentence in correct order using what we know about syntax rules and the present progressive verb tense.

Guided reconstruction steps:

1. Find the possible verbs. (is, practice, observing) Which two verbs can go together? ("is observing")
2. Find the possible subjects. (court, coach, athletes, they)
3. Match the subjects to verbs. ("coach is observing" and "athletes/they practice")
4. Find possible adjectives. (the, the, the)
5. Match adjectives to nouns. ("the court" "the coach" "the athletes")
6. Find possible prepositions. (on)
7. Match prepositions to nouns/noun phrases. ("on the court")
8. Find possible conjunctions. (while)
9. Match clauses using the conjunction.

Shuffles *(That address verb tense and grammatical features.)*	New Sentence
Shuffle 1: Simple Sentence	The coach is observing the athletes.
Shuffle 2: Negative	The coach is not observing the athletes.
Shuffle 3: Interrogative	Is the coach observing the athletes?
Shuffle 4: Move the clauses.	While they practice on the court, the coach is observing the athletes. OR While they practice, the coach is observing the athletes on the court.
Shuffle 5: Change to a plural subject.	On the court, the coaches are observing the athletes while they practice.

Possible shuffles: Change the preposition of location. Change the subordinating conjunction.

observing	they
court,	coach
the	On
practice.	while
the	the
is	athletes

During the Lesson

Step 1- Reveal the Mixed-Up Words

Introduce the lesson by explaining that students will look at a group of words that are out of order, but will make a complete sentence in English when reorganized. Assure that words are out of order and turn them over one at a time in a pocket chart or on the whiteboard as students read them. If students mispronounce or misread a word, help them. Remember though that this is *not* a vocabulary lesson. Spend no more than sixty seconds revealing all of the words in the sentence.

Step 2- Guided Reconstruction

This is the guided portion of the lesson that will enable students to work independently in the future. As a teacher, your goal is to lead students to the answer rather than giving it to them.

> 1. Start each reconstruction by asking,

> **Tip!**
> *Why call them "possible" verbs, subjects, and adjectives?*
> There are many words that can be used as verbs, nouns or adjectives depending on the syntax, such as "running." Make sure you look at more than just the ending when identifying parts of speech.

> **Tip!**
> *Why do we start with verbs?*
> Many teachers wonder why we start our reconstruction by looking for verbs rather than possible subjects since subjects generally precede verbs in sentence structure. Consider the following:
> - While English sentences require a subject and a verb, the subject is sometimes implied as in command sentences: *Go home. Sit down. Stop that.* Really, the only part of speech <u>needed</u> to form a complete sentence is a verb.
> - There are generally fewer conjugated verbs in a sentence than there are possible subjects (nouns and pronouns). Finding the conjugated verbs first gives you clues to the nature of the subject (singular or plural).

"What does every sentence need?" Students should be able to tell you that every sentence needs a subject and a verb.

2. As the verb is the center of the sentence, instruct students to find all possible verbs in the sentence. *Possible verbs are conjugated verbs and not verbs in the infinitive form.

3. Look for all of the possible subjects. Ask students what they are looking for when they search for subjects. Students should be able to tell you that a subject is either a noun or a pronoun. Find the

possible subjects and put them to the left of the verbs.

4. Instruct students to try to match the possible subjects to the conjugated verbs thus making clauses, or simple sentences. Point out to students that they now have simple sentences but are lacking details.

Tip!

What do I do with words like "and" and "or?"

If simple coordinating conjunctions are used to connect two subjects, two verbs, or other parts of speech, you can instruct students to join them using the coordinating conjunction when they find their subjects, verbs, or other parts of speech.

Try the prompting question:
"Is there any way we can connect these two

_____ *(nouns/pronouns/verbs/adjectives) so that they go together?"*

Your pocket chart should now look like this:

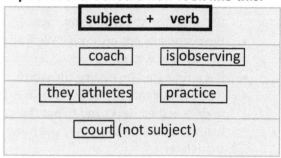

From this point on, the guided reconstruction steps will depend on the grammatical features present in the sentence.

5. Find the possible adjectives (includes articles). Match the possible adjectives to the nouns.

Your pocket chart should look like this:

6. Find the pronouns. Instruct students to match them to nouns they might replace. Point out to students that a pronoun is generally used after the noun is named.

7. Find the prepositions. Match them to nouns to create prepositional phrases.

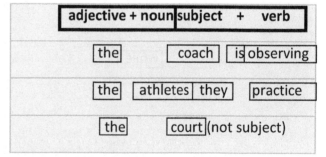

Your pocket chart should look like this:

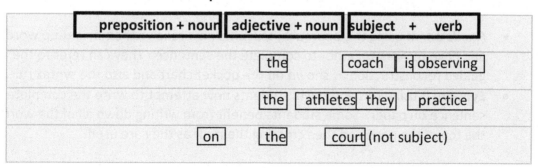

Tip!

Tips for Managing Student Completion of the Sentence

- Have materials ready: scissors, copies of words.
- Instruct students to *only* cut on the lines and not around the words or letter.
- Instruct students to cut the middle line first and then the horizontal lines.
- Have students cut with you. "We'll all say the word as we cut it."
- Put a time limit on cutting the words.
- Instruct students to place all words in the middle of their desks and to put the blanks to the side since they will need them later.
- Provide pre-cut words when you know that students will not have enough time to cut.

8. Find the conjunctions (especially subordinating conjunctions). If the sentence has more than one clause, use the conjunction to connect them.
9. Find the possible adverbs. Use them to describe the verbs, adjectives or adverbs in the sentence.

The sentence should _not_ be complete when you are finished guiding students through all the syntax rules. After you have led students through the syntax rules, they are ready to complete the sentence on their own or in groups.

This is what the pocket chart should look like before students are instructed to complete the sentence on their own.

Notice that the words have been joined to form phrases or clauses. Students must now put these phrases or clauses in order.

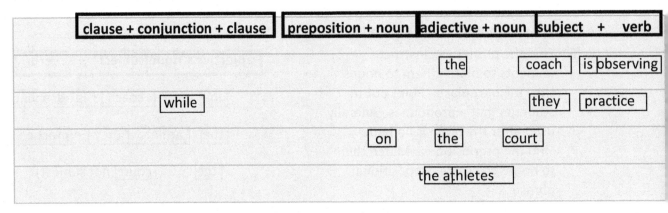

clause + conjunction + clause	preposition + noun	adjective + noun	subject + verb
		the	coach	is observing
while			they	practice
	on the court		
the athletes			

Step 3- Students Complete Sentence

- **Hands-on:** If using this approach, students now receive their mixed-up words and have to work together to complete the sentence. They can refer to the guided reconstruction as shown on the pocket chart and also the syntax rules.
- **Eyes-on:** If using this approach, students now attempt to write the complete sentence on paper. Some students benefit from writing down all of the words at the top of the page and then crossing them off as they are used.

<u>Step 4- Shuffles</u>

Provide at least one minute for all students to complete the sentence. When the sentence is complete, have students dictate it to you so that your sentence on the pocket chart now shows the original sentence. If students construct variations of the original sentence, validate the grammatically correct sentences and provide guidance on the incorrect versions.

You are now ready to start the "Shuffles" of *Syntax Surgery*. Plan for at least five shuffles every time and always have students change the form of the sentences. If using a sentence with more than one clause or with prepositional phrases, consider having students shorten the sentence as the first shuffle.

1. **Shorten the sentence:**
   a. Ask students to identify the subject in the sentence (Students can hold up the piece(s) of paper with the subject.)
   b. Ask students to identify the main verb/verb phrase in the sentence.
   c. Ask students again what two parts sentences need to be complete (They should tell you that sentences need a subject and a verb.)
   d. Instruct students to remove the extra details from their sentences leaving only the main clause. Leave certain aspects like articles in the complete subject or direct objects to maintain the meaning in the main clause.

2. **Negative form:** If the original sentence was in the declarative form, have students change it to the negative form. Be sure to have pieces of paper ready with any words you might need to add or change in the sentence (not, etc.). Allow students to first change the sentence and then make your sentence match theirs by asking them for directions on how to change the sentence to the negative form.
3. **Interrogative form:** Ask students to now change the sentence to the interrogative form. After students have completed this shuffle, they can instruct you on how to change the teacher sentence.

Additional Shuffles

Before introducing any other shuffles, have students first put the original sentence back together if they have only been working with the simple sentence.

- **Change the subject:** If changing the subject from singular to plural or plural to singular will affect the form of the verb, have students change the subject by flipping it over and writing a new subject on the back. Prompt students with, "Is the subject singular or plural and how do you know?" If students don't automatically change the verb, encourage them to look for something else in the sentence that will also have to change.

- **Move a phrase or clause elsewhere in the sentence:** Have students locate phrases or clauses by asking, "Which part of the sentence tells us _____ (where/when/why/how)?" and then, "Is there any other place that we can move this part of the sentence?." Students should see that as long as the subject and verb remain together, the other details in the sentence can often be moved.

- **Change the tense of the sentence:** First have students identify the tense of the sentence and explain how they know. Then ask students to change the tense of the sentence to a tense that they have previously practiced. This is a great way to review former tenses, but don't forget to have at least the formula for the specified tense accessible for student use.

- **Replace a key word with a synonym:** If you used a key vocabulary word or a new word in the sentence that you would like students to practice, ask them to replace the word with a synonym by flipping the word over and writing a new word.

- **Replace a key word with another word from the same part of speech:** If you would like your students to practice more with a particular part of speech, instruct them to flip a particular word over and replace it with a word from the same part of speech. Students should be able to use the *Grammar Wall* for this shuffle.

- **Add a new feature to the sentence:** Perhaps you would like students to add an adverb or make a compound subject. Ask them to use one of their blank pieces of paper and write the specified part of speech before adding it to the sentence.

Assessment

Student proficiency for the syntax rules they have practiced can be assessed in the following ways:

- ✓ Take an "Eyes-on" sentence and have students construct the sentence and complete the "Shuffles" independently.
- ✓ Provide students with a mixed-up sentence that is structurally similar to a previously practiced sentence and have them reconstruct it on their own.
- ✓ Ask students to write down the syntax rules they used in reconstructing a sentence.
- ✓ Provide students with a complete sentence and ask them to perform various shuffles.
- ✓ Provides students with a complete sentence and ask them to place the words on the Grammar Wall while justifying the placement by saying how they know.
- ✓ Take a sentence from a previous *Verb Tense Study* and have students design their own *Syntax Surgery* lesson.
- ✓ Ask pairs or groups of students to lead the class through the reconstruction of a sentence.
- ✓ For an extra challenge, provide students with the mixed-up words from more than one sentence and have them reconstruct all sentences.

Tip!

Fun Ways to Finish the Lesson

- **Human Sentence:** Pass out words from the original teacher sentence and have students stand in front of the class with the words arranged in the correct order.
- **Add Words to the *Grammar Wall*:** Pass out words to students and ask them to place them on the *Grammar Wall* telling what part of speech the word is and how they know.
- **Syntax Steps Review:** Ask students to dictate or write down the syntax rules they used and the order in which they followed them. This will lead to increased proficiency in future lesson or for independent practice.

What *Syntax Surgery* looks like across the language levels

Syntax Surgery can be completed with any language level though the number of syntax rules used, the length of the sentence, and the level of the words can vary by level. Use the chart below for some basic guidelines.

sentence/level	Beginner	Intermediate	Advanced
number of syntax rules used	-two to four	-five to six	-more than six
verb tense utilized	-any practiced in a previous *Verb Tense Study*	-any practiced in a previous *Verb Tense Study*	-any practiced in a previous *Verb Tense Study*
length of sentence	5-10 words	10-15 words	15+ words
parts of speech that start each sentence	-nouns -pronouns -articles	-no articles -no subject pronouns -adjectives -prepositions -adverbs	-adverbs -prepositions -conjunctions -gerunds
types of shuffles	-negative -interrogative -change the subject -identify nouns, verb, adjectives, and replace them -replace key words with synonyms	-negative -interrogative -change the subject -replace key words with synonyms -move clauses or phrases to different parts of the sentence -replace key words with other words from the same part of speech -change the tense of the sentence	-negative -interrogative -change the subject -replace key words with synonyms -move clauses or phrases to different parts of the sentence -replace key words with other words from the same part of speech -change the tense of the sentence -add another feature to the sentence

What this Method *Isn't*

It's <u>not</u> a vocabulary guessing game. The objective of the lesson is neither to learn new vocabulary words nor is it to put words together based on what "sounds right."

It's <u>not</u> an unsupervised puzzle in which students haphazardly link words together without feedback.

It's <u>not</u> the time to use a simple sentence that students can complete before even seeing all of the words. The level of the *Syntax Surgery* sentence should match the level of guided sentences completed in the *Verb Tense Study*.

It's <u>not</u> a race to see who can complete the sentence before the teacher has guided students through the syntax rules. For this reason, don't pass out the student words until after the Guided Reconstruction during a "Hands-on" lesson.

Things to Re-think

1. Because many of us have come to speak a language without formal language instruction, how has that affected our views and approaches for helping English learners to master English syntax?
2. Is it possible that overt teaching of sentence structure could actually accelerate and complement human's natural tendency to learn languages?
3. English learners stuck at the "intermediate" level of English proficiency comprise, in most states, more than two thirds of all English learners. What do these students have to teach us about the role of explicit grammar teaching?
4. Is teaching "in English" really the same as "teaching" English? Which is actually a planned instructional program?

Administrators' Corner

<u>What to look for in *Syntax Surgery*</u>

→ Is the method clearly labeled?

→ Is there a Preview Chart readily accessible for student reference?

→ Can all students easily read the words in the sentence from where they are seated?

→ Is there a set of syntax rules somewhere near the sentence?

→ Is the teacher guiding students through the syntax rules *before* having students complete the sentence on their own?

→ Are students able to verbalize the syntax rules they are using?

→ Can students justify their placement of words in the sentence?

→ Are words being added to the *Grammar Wall* at the end of the lesson?

→ Are both the teacher and the students avoiding the justifications of "It sounds right." or, "It makes sense."

→ Do classrooms of different language levels show different levels of student production?

5. Is it possible that teachers don't know enough about English grammar to make direct instruction of English grammar a realistic possibility?

What to Expect

➢ You are going to learn about asking grammar questions. The usual tendency for teachers new to this method is to ask lots of *what* questions. *What is this part of speech? What does the verb do? What kind of sentence is this?* Try to avoid *what* questions, as they don't lend themselves to the level of analysis we are striving for with this method. Questions that start with *what* also allow students to answer with only one or two words. A better way to question during this method uses *how*. *How do you know this word is a verb?*

➢ Use your *Grammar Wall* as a resource, for both you and the students. Much like a number line in mathematics, a solidly built *Grammar Wall* can keep you moving along without having to over-rely on memory of grammar concepts.

➢ Students will want to put the sentence together quickly and collect the $1 million first prize. This is not a race, but rather a mediated social context in which students are learning how language is constructed. Remember, the analysis *is* the method.

➢ Decide whether you will provide students with the words already written and cut up, or whether that is a task they can do for themselves. Use sandwich bags to store the words, use different color ink so you can quickly keep like sentences together, and use a pocket chart for your portion of the method.

➢ Be prepared for some students to want to revert back to the Old View and the comfort of that world. For it was there that rules did not matter, structure was an accessory, and accuracy happened largely by chance. You are teaching grammar in a way that will open up new literacy panoramas for your students. Help them to see this brave new world.

Voices from the Classroom

Syntax Surgery is the best method since sentence diagramming. Seriously, it's a method that helps students manipulate the different parts of speech and develop the complexity of sentences. Students really enjoy this so much. They create their own versions to challenge the class. -Kevin from Madera, CA.

Using Syntax Surgery has changed the entire way I look at sentences and how I teach sentence writing to my students. Syntax Surgery has helped my EL students break sentences into smaller bits, and then teaches them how those parts can move around a sentence. –Ian from Madera, CA

Writing

Old View

As we have seen so far, there are substantial differences between what we have been calling the Old View and the New View for helping English learners to master the English language. Among the many contrasts, writing provides another view into how we have typically taught English learners versus what can be done to actually improve their linguistic repertoire. Let's examine briefly the two different lenses through which we can develop writing.

First, the Old View:

- Writing is the last domain for students to learn, following the listening-speaking-reading-writing order.

- Writing is developmental, and we should not expect grammatical accuracy from English learners until some point in the future.

- Expressing one's thoughts is the most important metric for writing, so it a native speaker can make sense of the student's writing, that passes as acceptable writing.

- The more writing students do, the better writers they will become.

- Process-writing approaches work best for English learners because of the iterative nature of revising, including reliance on peer editing.

- Editing a piece of writing for grammar can cause English learners to write less and to take fewer chances.

- Focusing on sentence accuracy can detract writers from getting their true ideas onto paper.

New View

By contrast, the New View of writing instruction for English learners draws on a different set of precepts.

- Writing should be taught simultaneously with the other language domains (listening, speaking, reading).

- Students should be provided grammatically indexed topics to write about for which their English grammar skills are sufficient.

- Students should first have control over writing sentences before moving to paragraphs and other more complex ways of organizing written discourse, e.g., research papers, argumentation, compare and contrast test structures, etc.

- The use of formulas for constructing sentences and paragraphs serves to move English learners systematically from simple to complex forms of writing.

- Content expression cannot be separated from grammatical accuracy; in the real world, both are viewed as a whole—and sometimes viewed harshly.

- Teacher mediation plays a huge role in helping students to synthesize their grammar skills, sentence writing skills and content knowledge into a coherent whole.

In a nutshell, the Old View exhorts teachers to have English learners write—and write some more—on topics that cover the content rainbow. The New View holds that writing skills develop hierarchically based on control of learned language skills and structures. Both views have tremendous implications when it comes to academic content and what teachers expect students to know and be able to do with language in its written form.

Reading Comprehension Connection

One of the most flagrant paradoxes in the daily academic life of an English learner is the huge disparity in language complexity between what they are asked to "read" and what they are actually able to write. Most fifth-grade textbooks feature sentences that average around 15 words per sentence, with many sentences exceeding 25 words. Naturally, these sentences use all eight parts of speech in ways that serve to convey meaning, tone, authority, and clarity. Most authors deliberately vary their sentence structure, use exciting new vocabulary, and try to keep the reader's attention by avoiding word redundancy and offering up intriguing grammatical flourishes. By contrast, English learners who have lived the Old View are bound by a few simple sentence patterns they use repeatedly, a stock index of tried and true words, and a limited—if not non-existent—ability to vary their language use in ways that sound learned and erudite. The paradox is that they are exposed all day long to books loaded with sophisticated grammar constructions that they are expected to comprehend. These sentences in text are so radically different than what students can do with language that comprehension breaks down early and often. At its illogical conclusion, they are diagnosed with "reading comprehension problems" when what they really suffer from is *few-sentence-pattern-itis*, a malady that can be cured not by more "reading," but by actually learning more of the grammar patterns that show up in their texts.

Academic Writing Connection

Visit most classrooms of any grade level that are populated by English learners and look at posted writing samples from those students. Here is what you are likely to find:

- Writing dominated by the simple subject pronouns I and You
- Sentences that frequently—if not always—start with a subject followed by a simple verb
- Organizational issues that make "flow" elusive, even for a native English speaker reading the text
- A preponderance of writing that is in first person, whether by assignment or by the student's regression to their most comfortable point of view
- Many short sentences joined by the conjunctions *and* or *because*
- Abundant and consistent grammar errors mottled with misspellings and strange word choices

Go back to the classroom in a month, or three months, and you will usually see minimal growth in writing skills though there may be more samples of writing and they may be longer in length. Stay long enough to watch the writing instruction and you are likely to see a teacher review a literary or mechanical aspect of writing, e.g. exhortations to use more metaphors, hot tips on describing words, or reminders about indenting and the use of capitals and periods. After the mini-lecture, students will bow their heads and begin "writing." In most cases, they will do again what they have always done.

The method you are about to learn is what would properly be called in an academic setting a *mediated* method, and it derives from theoretical ideas about language learning developed by Lev Vygotsky in the early part of the 20th century. In short, you will see at least two very different aspects to writing instruction in the New View classroom: the role of the teacher and the role of assigned grammar structures that guide the writing. You will learn how teachers must establish before the lesson a *Desired Linguistic Outcome,* so that both you and the students know what language skills are essential to the text construction process. And you will learn that the teacher's role in developing the writing of English learners is more like that of authoritative co-pilot than a simple assigner of prompts or a cheerleader who celebrates any symbol—never mind correctness—put to paper.

Students need to be capable of crafting relevant and academic sentences that correspond to sequenced pictures, writing prompts, and other academic writing tasks.

Method

Four-Picture Story Frames

Description

Students produce a paragraph compiled of sentences produced through the use of a picture prompt and writing frame.

Purpose

This method creates an interactive structure for teachers to assist students in developing organized writing that uses complex vocabulary, more advanced sentence structures, and transitional language words. For English learners, this method serves as a critical bridge between more structured language-learning methods and independent student writing.

Materials Needed

- ☐ a set of four related pictures
- ☐ chart paper
- ☐ markers
- ☐ sticky notes or magnetic index cards
- ☐ *Grammar Wall*

Teacher Skills

- ✓ familiarity with the *Grammar Wall*
- ✓ knowledge of how interrogative questions (who, what, where, when, how, why) link to specific parts of speech
- ✓ ability to write and prepare a cohesive paragraph
- ✓ ability to anticipate students' independent writing level and prepare for a higher level of production

Language Objective: We will write a paragraph in the _____ tense using precise vocabulary and advanced sentence structures.

Steps

This method can be done independently of other methods to instruct grammar usage in writing. However, students greatly benefit from the method when it is used after a *Verb Tense Study* lesson. Once students have learned how and why to use a particular verb tense, they can practice the tense's application during the writing practice offered in *Four-Picture Story Frames*.

Four-Picture Story Frames - Steps at a Glance

Preparation	*Procedures*

Preparation

1. Select four pictures that used together could illustrate a story or paragraph.

2. Plan a desired linguistic outcome- the ideal paragraph that you would want students to generate.
   a. Write the syntax pattern for each sentence.

3. Prepare four pieces of chart paper by writing interrogatives to be used on each (examples on following pages).

4. Prepare sticky notes or magnetic index cards for each of the interrogatives to be used.

5. Have a recently completed *Verb Tense Study* nearby as the formula will be used.

6. Ensure that your *Grammar Wall* has the interrogatives posted where they belong and sufficient example words under each.

Procedures

1. Show pictures out of order. Ask students what the pictures are about.
2. Students sequence the pictures.

*For the first lesson, attach the interrogatives to the Grammar Wall before moving on.

3. **Picture #1**
   - Generate "who."
   - Generate "what."
     o Select "who" and "what" for sentence.
     o Orally form simple sentence.
   - Generate other details.
     o where/when
     o why/how
   - Teacher selects components for details.
   - Teacher selects syntax pattern.
     o Start with "who" and "what."
     o Add the other interrogatives to the end of the sentence.
     o Change the order of the interrogatives (optional).
   - Students orally produce the sentence.
     o Teacher and students write the sentence.
   - Analysis of the sentence (It should match the *Verb Tense Study* formula.)
   - Students write a sentence independently.

4. **Picture #2** (Repeat procedure.)
5. **Picture #3** (Repeat procedure.)
6. **Picture #4** (Repeat procedure.)
7. Rewrite sentences to form a paragraph.
8. *Edit and Revise*

Discussion of Steps

Before the lesson begins

Step 1-Select four pictures

The four selected pictures will guide your students in producing four sentences to form a paragraph. Anything you can write about in a paragraph, you can use in *Four-Picture Story Frames*. Consider what topic you would like students to write about and then search for associated pictures. Here are a few ideas from different content areas and routines.

science	social studies	language arts	holidays	school routines
life cycles	event timeline	narrative plot	carving a pumpkin	getting ready for school
stages of erosion	biographical events	character traits	building a snowman	meeting with a counselor
water cycle	causes leading to event	cause and effect	decorating a tree	passing to the next class/level
food chain		setting description	making a feast	
animal traits				classroom rules
weather events				

When selecting pictures, choose colored photos or illustrations that can be easily seen by the entire class.

Step 2-Write the desired linguistic outcome

This is the lesson plan for your instruction. Now that you have four pictures, think about the paragraph that you will want students to write. For each picture, draft a target sentence and note the syntax pattern. A blank lesson template is shown on the following pages. We will discuss how to complete it.

Lesson Plan Template

Time Period: Past   Present   Future

Verb Tense(s): _____

Key Grammatical Features: _____

Paragraph (Desired Linguistic Output)

Who (Subject)	How	What (Infinitive Verb)

When	Why	Where

Sentence #1		Syntax Pattern

Who (Subject)		How		What (Infinitive Verb)	
When		Why		Where	
Sentence #2				Syntax Pattern	

Who (Subject)		How		What (Infinitive Verb)	
When		Why		Where	
Sentence #3				Syntax Pattern	

Who (Subject)	How	What (Infinitive Verb)

When	Why	Where

Sentence #4	Syntax Pattern

Revised Paragraph

Completing the Lesson Plan

Time Period: Select the time period in which students will write their paragraphs (past, present). Different tenses within each time period can be used.

Verb Tenses: Decide which tenses within the time period students will use. Consider recently studied tenses and only use tenses that students have already practiced.

Key Grammatical Features: Consider which, if any, grammatical structures students have recently studied. This method provides a great opportunity to practice those structures in written application.

Language Objective: The language objective will always be to produce a paragraph using varied sentence structure and detailed sentences. However, the topic of the sentence and the verb tenses used will change with each paragraph.

Sentences

For each picture, write one sentence that can be broken into the associated interrogatives. Tying grammar to writing requires that both the teacher and the students understand which parts of speech answer which questions. The diagram below illustrates how sentences are structured as well as the parts of speech that can be used for each.

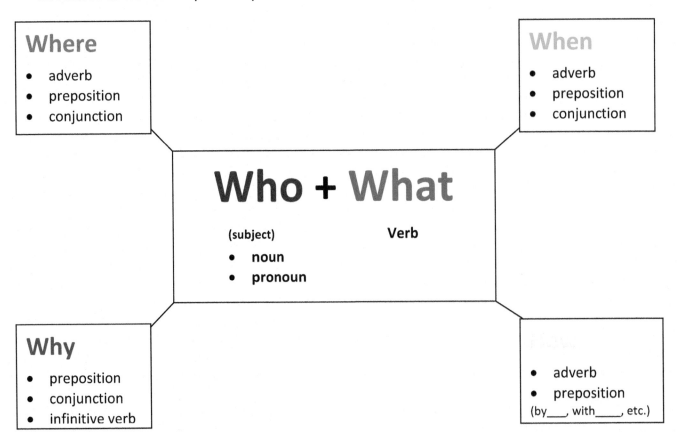

At the center of every sentence is the subject and verb telling who and what. Every other question (where, when, why, and how) is used to provide detail about the who and what. Understanding this makeup helps students not only to write in complete sentences but also to strategically add detail.

In completing the lesson plan, think of the *who* and *what* for each sentence and then add details to answers one or more of the other interrogatives. An example is provided below.

> Who: Whales
> What: to migrate

Simple sentence: **Whales migrate.**

> Where: to warmer waters
> When: when the weather gets colder
> Why: for mating and breeding

Sentence with detail:
When the weather gets colder, whales migrate to warmer waters for mating and breeding.

Syntax Pattern:
When + Who + What + Where + Why

> ### Tip!
> ### When the "What" is more than an infinitive verb
>
> Verbs answer the question, "What?" for each sentence. Some verbs are intransitive, meaning they don't require an object (noun/pronoun) after, like "to migrate," "to sit," and "to meditate."
>
> Other verbs, transitive verbs, do require objects after them, such as "to produce____," "to accept____," and "to donate____." When using transitive verbs, include the object as part of the "what." Drawing a blank line after the verb can signal to students that they must use an object to complete the "what."

Once the sentence is written, write the syntax pattern to the right in the "syntax pattern" box. (The syntax pattern is the order in which the writer answers the interrogatives.) Then, write each component of the sentence under the interrogative that it answers. Because students will be writing their own sentences after the collaborative writing, you can also think about another option to answer each interrogative.

Part of the goal is to write detailed sentences. Try answering at least one or two of the interrogatives for each sentence. Remember that not every sentence has to answer every interrogative.

A completed sample lesson plan is provided on the following pages.
The *Edit and Revise* portion of the lesson will be discussed at the end of the steps.

Four-Picture Story Frames

Sample Lesson Plan

Time Period: Past   ⬭Present⬭   Future

Verb Tense(s): Simple Present _____

Key Grammatical Features: _____

Language Objective: We will produce a paragraph about the life cycle of frogs using:

- the simple present tense
- detailed sentences
- varied sentence structure

Paragraph (Desired Linguistic Output)
During the spring, the mother frog lays thousands of tiny eggs on the surface of the water. The tadpoles swim through the water to find food after they have hatched. Slowly over the next few weeks, the young froglets develop legs and lungs so that they can live on land. Because they have fully developed lungs and legs after 12-16 weeks, the adult frogs successfully live on land and swim in the water.

Who (Subject)	How	What (Infinitive Verb)
the mother frog	x	to lay <u>thousands of tiny eggs</u>
tiny eggs	x	to develop
When	**Why**	**Where**
during the spring	x	on the surface of the water
in the first stage of the life cycle	x	near the riverbank
Sentence #1		**Syntax Pattern**
During the spring, the mother frog lays thousands of eggs on the surface of the water.		When + Who + What + Where

Who (Subject)	How	What (Infinitive Verb)
tadpoles	X	to swim
recently hatched tadpoles	X	to search for _____
When	**Why**	**Where**
in the second stage of life	because they are hungry	through the water
after they have hatched	to find food	throughout the pond
Sentence #2		**Syntax Pattern**
Tadpoles swim through the water to find food after they have hatched.		Who + What + Where + Why + When

Who (Subject)	How	What (Infinitive Verb)
the young froglets	slowly	to mature
the juvenile frogs	gradually	to develop _____(both legs and lungs)
When	**Why**	**Where**
over the next few weeks	in order to survive on land	x
in the next stage of life	so that they can breathe and move on land	x
Sentence #3		**Syntax Pattern**
Slowly over the next few weeks, the young froglets develop both legs and lungs so that they can breathe and move on land.		How + When + Who + What + Why

Who (Subject)	How	What (Infinitive Verb)
the adult frogs	with fully developed lungs and legs	to have _____ (developed lungs and legs)
fully matured frogs	successfully	to live, to swim
When	**Why**	**Where**
after 12-16 weeks	because they have fully developed lungs and legs	on land
in the final stage of life	because they have matured	in the water
Sentence #4		**Syntax Pattern**
Because they have fully developed lungs and legs after 12-16 weeks, the adult frogs successfully live on land and swim in the water.		Why + When + Who + How + What + Where + What + Where

---

Revised Paragraph

   Frogs have four stages in their life cycle. During the spring, the mother frog egg lays thousands of tiny eggs on the surface of the pond. After they've hatched, the tadpoles swim through the water to find food.   Slowly over the next few weeks, the young froglets develop legs and lungs so that they can live on land. Because their development is complete after 12-16 weeks, the adult frogs successfully live on land and swim in the water.

Step 3- Prepare four pieces of chart paper

Each sentence and picture goes on its own piece of chart paper. Label each piece of chart paper with the interrogatives that will be answered.

Example

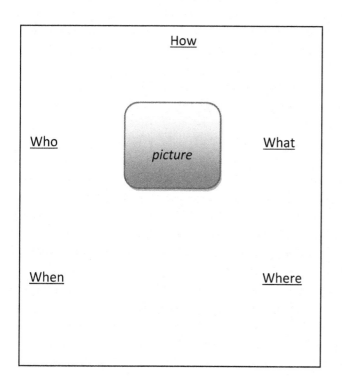

Tip!

Pencil in the components of the desired linguistic outcome under each interrogative so that you don't have to refer to your notes during the lesson. You can also pencil in the syntax pattern.

Step 4-Preparing the interrogatives to be used

The interrogatives for the syntax pattern are best displayed on sticky notes or magnetic index cards so that they can be moved and manipulated throughout the lesson. Students should be able to see that the details continually revolve around the center of the sentence, the who and the what.

Remember that not all sentences will answer each interrogative and other sentences can answer each interrogative more than once. Have at least two of each interrogative on hand.

Who	What	Where	When	Why	How

Step 5-The verb tense formula

Make sure that the *Verb Tense Study* preview chart(s) for the tense(s) that students will be using are nearby so that students can reference the formula.

Step 6-The prepared *Grammar Wall*

The interrogatives serve not only to guide students in adding more detail to their sentences but also to show students the link between writing and grammar. The same interrogatives used in the *Four-Picture Story Frames* method should also be posted on the *Grammar Wall* near the parts of speech that answer them. The following illustration shows the link between the parts of speech and the interrogatives they answer.

Adjectives *Who*	Nouns (subject) *Who*	Pronouns (subject) *Who*	Verbs *What*
(used to describe nouns and pronouns)			
Adverbs *How* of manner *Where* *When* of direction of time/ frequency	Prepositions *Why* of purpose *Where* *When* of location of time	Conjunctions *When* *Why* of time of cause	Interjections *Wow!*

> **Tip!**
>
> Having the interrogatives labeled on the *Grammar Wall* is only the first step. There must be sample words beneath each interrogative under the different parts of speech also!
>
> Consider some of the more challenging words that you would like students to utilize during the *Four-Picture Story Frames* method. Planting a few of the words on the *Grammar Wall* before the lesson is a great way to get students to both use the *Grammar Wall* and more advanced vocabulary. The *Grammar Wall* not only shows which words to use, but **how** to use them.

During the Lesson

Step 1- Show pictures out of order.

Introduce the lesson by explaining that students will use the set of pictures to write a paragraph. Show the pictures to students and have them discuss the main idea from the set of pictures. This step will assure that students are thinking along the same lines for paragraph construction.

Step 2- Students sequence the pictures.

Collaboratively, students order the pictures from first to last. This is a small step that should take less than one minute.

*For the first lesson, ask students to identify which parts of speech answer which questions. Example: "Which parts of speech tell us 'when?'"

Step 3-Picture #1

Attach the first picture to the first piece of chart paper.

1. Generate two-three answers for the "who" by asking students to share possible "who's" with their partner.

2. Generate two-three answers for the "what" by asking students to share possible "what's" with their partner.

   a. The teacher selects the who and what that students will be using to create their sentence. This will allow students to focus the other details on giving more information about the who and the what, the essential clause of the sentence.

   b. Students orally combine the subject and the verb to both practice conjugating the verb and also to form the center of the sentence to which details will now be added.

3. Generate other details by asking questions using the main clause: "Where do whales migrate?" "When do whales migrate?" Continue the same procedure with the other interrogatives. When first implementing the lesson, consider how many of the interrogatives you are going to use. Have students practice adding where and when before attempting how and why.

4. Teacher selects the other components of the sentence (by circling or marking with a star, etc.) The example on the next page shows what your chart should look like at this point.

The chart should now look like this.

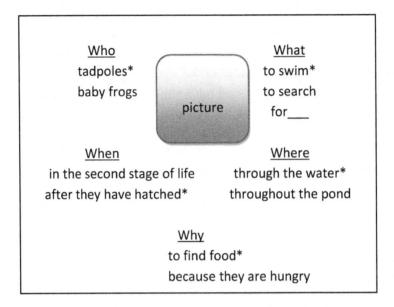

Who
tadpoles*
baby frogs

What
to swim*
to search
for___

picture

When
in the second stage of life
after they have hatched*

Where
through the water*
throughout the pond

Why
to find food*
because they are hungry

5. Teacher selects syntax pattern using interrogative sticky notes or index cards.

   a. Start with the who and the what and have students form the simple sentence using the indicated verb tense. Refer students to the completed *Verb Tense Study* charts and have them decide how to correctly conjugate the verb.

   b. Now add other interrogatives to the end of the sentence to add more detail.

   c. Finally, you can show students how components other than the subject can be moved to the beginning of the sentence to suit the author's purpose.

   Tip!
   Students should be able to orally produce the sentence *without the teacher reading along* at each step after the syntax pattern has been provided.

6. Students orally produce the sentence.

   a. Once students have shown that they are fluent with the sentence, they can write it in their journals or loose paper.

   b. The teacher also writes the sentence on the chart paper.

7. Students analyze the sentence to assure that it matches the verb tense formula indicated. Have students identify both the subject and the verb.

8. Students now write their own sentences in their journals. They should follow the same syntax pattern but can use other components from the chart or their own

The chart should now look like this.

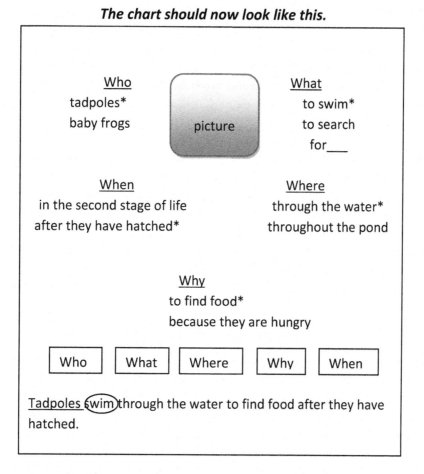

Steps 4, 5, 6-Pictures #2, #3, #4

Repeat the same procedures done with picture #1 until all four charts are complete.

Step 7- Form a paragraph

Rewrite all four sentences on one piece of chart paper to form a paragraph. Leave room between lines to allow for revisions.

Step 8-*Edit and Revise*

Edit and Revise is a procedure that can be used with any student writing. Although it's the final step for *Four-Picture Story Frames*, it is a lesson on its own. For this reason, we will more fully discuss the steps for the *Edit and Revise* procedure with examples below.

The following steps are for the teacher to guide students through one written piece for collaborative revisions. A student sheet follows.

> **Step 1:** Re-read the writing and correct any obvious errors such as missing words, capitalization, or punctuation.
>
> **Step 2:** Circle all the conjugated verbs.
>
> > a. Is it conjugated? (Not the infinitive = "to" + verb)
> >
> > > i. Possible endings: -s, -es, -ing, -ed
> > >
> > > ii. Modal form: modal + base verb
> > >
> > > iii. Don't forget the "to be" verbs!
> >
> > b. Does it follow the subject?
> >
> > c. Does the subject perform the action of the verb?

The chart should now look like this.

> During the spring, the mother frog (lays) thousands of eggs on the surface of the water. The tadpoles (swim) through the water to find food after they (have hatched) Slowly over the next few weeks, the young froglets (develop) legs and lungs so that they (can live) on land. Because they (have) fully developed lungs and legs after 12-16 weeks, the adult frogs successfully (live) on land and (swim) in the water.

> **Step 3:** Do the conjugated verbs show cohesion?
>
> > a. Are they in one tense?
> >
> > b. Do they logically flow from one tense to another?
> >
> > > i. Past to present to future= yes!
> > >
> > > ii. Present to past = yes!
> > >
> > > iii. Present to past to present = no!

If the tenses are not cohesive, select which tense you will use and assure that all verbs are in that tense.

Step 4: Box all the subjects. Using the organizer on the student sheet, write out the subjects and the main verbs of each sentence. Do they agree? (Refer students to the Preview Chart of the correlating *Verb Tense Study* to verify that the subject and verb agree.) Do the subjects and verbs show a logical order to the paragraph?

The chart should now look like this.

During the spring, the mother frog lays thousands of eggs on the surface of the water. The tadpoles swim through the water to find food after they have hatched. Slowly over the next few weeks, the young froglets develop legs and lungs so that they can live on land. Because they have fully developed lungs and legs after 12-16 weeks, the adult frogs successfully live on land and swim in the water.

Step 5: Read consecutive sentences for "flow."

- a. Do particular syntax elements flow?
    - i. Where: in Brazil, across Antarctica= no!
    - ii. Where: from the Brazilian coast, toward Antarctica= yes!
- b. Are transitions needed?
    - i. Answering "when" at the beginning of a sentence often allows for flow.
    - ii. If the setting (when or where) changes between sentences, start the second sentence by introducing the new "when" or "where."
    - iii. Conjunctive adverbs link sentences.
- c. Is an introductory or concluding sentence needed?

The chart should now look like this.

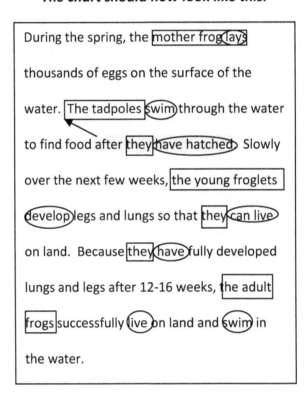

During the spring, the mother frog lays thousands of eggs on the surface of the water. The tadpoles swim through the water to find food after they have hatched. Slowly over the next few weeks, the young froglets develop legs and lungs so that they can live on land. Because they have fully developed lungs and legs after 12-16 weeks, the adult frogs successfully live on land and swim in the water.

Step 6: Underline any word that appears more than twice.

    a. Is there a better word that can replace the repetition?

        i. Determine pronouns or synonyms that could replace the repeated words or phrases.

        ii. Would a native, proficient English speaker have used a different word?

    b. Don't worry about articles, prepositions or technical terms.

The chart should now look like this.

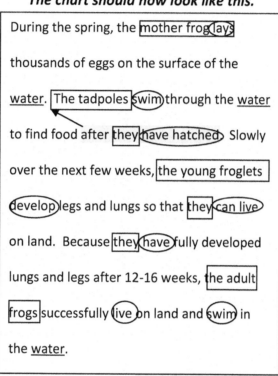

During the spring, the mother frog lays thousands of eggs on the surface of the water. The tadpoles swim through the water to find food after they have hatched. Slowly over the next few weeks, the young froglets develop legs and lungs so that they can live on land. Because they have fully developed lungs and legs after 12-16 weeks, the adult frogs successfully live on land and swim in the water.

Step 7: Check the syntax patterns.

    a. Is there a variety of syntax patterns? If not, where can a new element be added?

Step 8: Re-read and correct any misspellings or other errors. Make any final stylistic changes.

Step 9: Rewrite the paragraph including all revisions and corrections.

The chart should now look like this. (Final paragraph)

> Frogs have four stages in their life cycle.
>
> During the spring, the mother frog lays thousands of tiny eggs on the surface of the pond. After they've hatched, the tadpoles swim through the water to find food. Slowly over the next few weeks, the young froglets develop legs and lungs so that they can live on land. Because their development is complete after 12-16 weeks, the adult frogs successfully live on land and swim in the water.

The following page is a template for students to use when editing and revising and written work.

EDIT AND REVISE

Name: _____   Date: _____ Period: _____

(1) VERB TENSES: → Are they cohesive?				(2) SUBJECTS AND VERBS: → Do they agree?

(1) VERB TENSES:
→ Are they cohesive?

Verb	Past	Present	Future

(2) SUBJECTS AND VERBS:
→ Do they agree?

Subject   *Verb*

_____ | _____
_____ | _____
_____ | _____
_____ | _____

(3) REPETITION:
→ Rule of Two!

Old Word ⟶ *New Word*

_____ ⟶
_____ ⟶
_____ ⟶
_____ ⟶

(4) ACCURACY/FLOW:
→ Do the subjects and verbs fit together?
→ Read two consecutive sentences together. Do we need to move a syntax element or add a transition to improve flow?

Assessment

Student proficiency for writing using the picture frames can be assessed in the following ways.

    ✓ Pass out four pictures and students independently create a paragraph by using the picture frames.

    ✓ Collaboratively generate the webbing for each picture, but then ask students to write the paragraph on their own.

    ✓ Have students edit and revise a completed paragraph.

    ✓ Ask students to manipulate the syntax pattern of a sentence to improve the flow.

    ✓ Instruct students to write a paragraph and set a minimum on the numbers of interrogatives they must answer per sentence.

    ✓ Students identify the syntax pattern for a written work.

What *Four-Picture Story Frames* looks like across the language levels

Four-Picture Story Frames can be completed with any language level. However, there are several components that will vary depending on student proficiency.

component/level	Beginner	Intermediate	Advanced
number of pictures and frames	-one to two	-three to four	-four or more
number of interrogatives/frame	-two-four	-three-five	-four-six
length of sentence	5-10 words	10-15 words	15+ words
tenses used	-one tense (usually the most recently studied)	-one-two (both previously studied)	-two or more *Students should strategically select from all the tenses they know.
level of independence	-75% collaborative	-50% collaborative	-25% collaborative

What this Method _Isn't_

It's <u>not</u> a vocabulary list. The object is not to list as many outputs as possible for each interrogative. Two to three high-level outputs are sufficient.

It's <u>not</u> a copying task. While the first few lessons may be completely collaborative, students should start moving toward more independence in their writing as they advance.

It's <u>not</u> the time to introduce a new grammar concept or verb tense. Students should be applying tenses and grammar concepts that they have _already_ learned for this method.

It's <u>not</u> independent writing. In this method, the teacher's job is to accelerate student language by pushing students to use words and structures that are more difficult. If students are able to complete the lesson independently, the lesson is too easy and needs to be revised. Remember, the teacher is the _mediator_ of higher-level language in this method.

It's <u>not</u> the time to teach content other than language. Students can use previously learned content, but new material in another content area should be taught separately. Remember that the objective of the lesson is _language_.

Things to Re-think

1. Why would teachers ask students to produce a piece of writing for which all parties (students and teacher) know that the students do not possess the language skills necessary?
2. Does doing any skill over and over again necessarily translate into more competence?

Administrators' Corner

<u>What to look for in _Four-Picture Story Frames_</u>

➔ Is the method clearly labeled?

➔ Do the four pictures show appropriate content for the grade and language level?

➔ Are there four picture frames on chart paper?

➔ Is there a _Verb Tense Study Preview Chart_ nearby with a clearly marked formula for students to reference?

➔ Is the _Grammar Wall_ labeled with the interrogatives?

➔ Are there sufficient words on the _Grammar Wall_ (at least 100) and under each interrogative for students to use?

➔ Are students asked to analyze the sentence after it's created?

➔ Are the sentences gathered into one paragraph (one piece of chart paper) at the end of the lesson?

➔ Do students use the _Edit and Revise_ process?

➔ Do students follow along in journals or on loose sheets of paper?

3. What are the risks for students and teachers when students practice the same mistakes?
4. Can you think of at least three new behaviors required of a teacher who uses this method?
5. In the absence of a *Desired Linguistic Outcome* established beforehand by the teacher, what might the finished product of this method look like?

What to Expect

➤ As with some of the other methods, your toughest critics are likely to be long-term English learners and other teachers. Students who have never seen this method, particularly those who are older and who have specialized in writing the same essay that they have written 200 times, will doubt its role and purpose. For some of your colleagues, it just looks, feels, and sounds different. You are actually writing with students with the goal of releasing them to write independently...weird. You already know what you want them to write, both language wise and content wise...really weird.

➤ Finding pictures can seem initially troublesome, but once your eyes and brain start looking, it is amazing how many picture sequences are readily available.

➤ Remind yourself that words organized correctly make sentences. This is the first step. Sentences organized logically make paragraphs. This is what we all want from students, so be patient with the initial formation of your sentences. Good stuff into the method usually translates into good stuff out of the method.

➤ Be prepared for your students to start viewing you as someone who is never happy with what they produce linguistically. Silently congratulate yourself for pushing students beyond what they can do independently as this is the essence of language acceleration and Vygotsky's life work.

Voices from the Classroom

Four-Picture Story Frames is tremendously helpful (and fun!) for me as a teacher. Students are able to visually see the relationship between actions, yet they are not able to articulate them in a second language. FPSF provides an opportunity for students to learn and practice transitional phrases, more complex syntax patterns, and incorporate multiple verb tenses. FPSF can be as simple or complex as the teacher desires and the students can handle. The sequential structuring of sentences as well as articulating the relationship between ideas is a huge step in helping English learners transition to essay writing. -Diane from Fresno, CA

I have found the Four-Picture Story Frames method to be an innovative way to effectively review cross-curricular content simultaneously with grammar instruction.

-Marisa from Cheshire, CT

Reading Methods

- *Text-cavation*

What empirical research supports a relationship between grammar knowledge and use and reading comprehension for second language learners?

Research over a period of nearly 90 years has consistently shown that the teaching of school grammar has little or no effect on students. – George Hillocks, 1991, in a publication of the National Council of Teachers of English.

Notwithstanding Mr. Hillocks' broad condemnation of grammar teaching, the fact remains that there is another side to the story. Starting with the general, a brief walk through the garden of research shows us some interesting findings when it comes to linking grammar instruction to reading comprehension *for second language learners*. Note that research about reading is abundant, even overwhelming. But that body of research deals primarily with the reading process for native speakers learning to read in their native language. Of course, our task with English learners is different. Still, it is perhaps axiomatic to assert that grammar must play some role in reading comprehension, or words could be sprinkled willy-nilly on a page with no deleterious effects on comprehension. Indeed, Koda (2007) points out the obvious: a readers' knowledge of grammar constrains the entire reading process. Global text comprehension, according to Koda, can be severely impaired if readers generate inaccurate and or/incomplete representations of the text.

The role of grammar in L2 reading, as previously mentioned, has not received as much attention by researchers relative to the volume of research on second language teaching and learning (Alderson, 1984; Nassaji, 2007; Shiotsu & Weir, 2007; Urquhart & Weir, 1998) or reading in general. Communicative approaches to language teaching beginning in the 1970s contributed to the lack of research interest. Bernhardt (2005) laments that over-adoption of L1 reading research in L2 reading studies overlooked the complexity of L2 reading.

Most studies addressing the grammar-reading comprehension relationship explored the issue by measuring the correlation between learners' L2 grammatical knowledge and their L2 reading comprehension (Urquhart & Weir, 1998). Alderson (1993) compared students' grammar and reading comprehension scores from a standardized test to draw correlations between the two, finding that higher grammar scores correlated with higher reading comprehension scores.

Several studies have tried to identify which aspects of reading (spelling, word recognition, vocabulary, background knowledge, etc.) most account for L2 readers' ability to comprehend L2 text (Barnett, 1986; Barry & Lazarte, 1995, 1998; Shiotsu & Weir, 2007). Barry and Lazarte (1995) conducted experiments that showed that syntactic complexity of sentence structures overruled the advantage of having text-related prior knowledge. Barnett's (1986) study explored the relative contributions to comprehension made by grammar and vocabulary to L2 reading comprehension and found that grammatical knowledge had as comparable an effect as that of vocabulary knowledge. Shiotsu and Weir (2007) found in their study that grammatical knowledge—defined as encompassing the knowledge of inflectional morphology, verb forms, and transformations—emerged as a stronger predictor of L2 reading ability than any other single element.

Reading Comprehension

Old View

One of the crowning achievements for a student learning a new language through the classical grammar-based theory and painful practice was to apply all of those isolated skills to reading. Indeed, the reading passages featured in foreign language textbooks were frequently controlled for grammar, making them "easier" to read and just more friendly. But what happened with alarming frequency was that the unsuspecting student kept finding new and unknown words in the text. And then the reach for the dictionary begins and the tiresome work of translating takes flight. The result is that the task moves from comprehension to one of tedious translation. For their efforts, the student ends up with a dog-eared dictionary and a collection of translated raindrops which together form only a muddy puddle of nothingness. Meaning, comprehension and enjoyment are essentially translated out of the text. With solid reason, the student asked himself and the grammar teacher a simple question: *What good was learning all of these discrete and disconnected grammar skills when, on the occasions that I try to use them, they do not help me to understand the text?* And so it goes...

As we have seen, grammar skills in the Classical Old View sometimes never made it to the application stage. Further, the skills seemed like tiny universes unto themselves, with little connection to other stars, planets, or universes. With so many tenuous links between them, the skills that comprise grammar took the blame: they were too onerous, too complex, too contradictory, too minute and there are just too many of them. The rules of grammar did little for the student who just wanted to read *Don Quixote* in its original Spanish version—and understand it.

Of course, the Old View 2.0 couldn't have espoused a more radical alternative: forget the little skills and focus on the big stuff, like comprehension, enjoyment, and interpretation of language and text. Some educational philosophers called it "making meaning," a term that was rarely defined but somehow had a general connotation of being good, worthwhile, useful, and culturally relevant. Strict, literal comprehension of text was eschewed in favor of having students "make meaning" because, after all, human beings are "meaning makers."

Reading became a "meaning-making transaction between a student and the text, or author." So out went the fixation with pieces of grammar and in came the love affair with "chunks;" large pieces of language that were said to carry more meaning and be more understandable and that required no learning of terms, rules, or function. So English learners were told by well-intentioned teachers to read for meaning. They opened their books and began to say words. But comprehension didn't always follow.

New View

Our New View again spans the chasm of both Old Views, asserting that learning and understanding a language taxonomy (read: eight parts of speech) can have an incredibly powerful and positive impact on reading comprehension and academic writing. But for grammar skills to find utility in these endeavors requires that we help students to see exactly how words function to create sentences, paragraphs, and meaning. Here are the precepts:

- The stock-in-trade interrogatives for talking about text in classrooms are as follows: *who, what, when, where, why,* and *how.* Teachers and tests ask questions of readers that invariably start with these question words.

- Each part of speech has a logical relationship to one or more of these interrogatives. If we ask *Who brought in the trash?*, we know from grammar that the subject of the response sentence will be either a noun or a pronoun. *George brought in the trash*, or *He brought in the trash*. If we want to discuss the *what*

of the sentence, we should look to the possible verbs and their position relative to the subject to tell us.

- By linking parts of speech to interrogatives, students see the function of words and how each category of words (nouns, verbs, conjunctions, etc.) serves to answer the various interrogatives.

- When we can find the *who, what, when, where, how,* and *why* in a sentence, and see their arrangement or order, we can talk about sentence patterns. Back to our example: *George brought in the trash.* Looked at from a syntax structure perspective, we can see that the simple formula is as follows: *Subject + verb + direct object.*

- By recognizing common sentence (or syntax) patterns in text, we can focus on the elements of a sentence that have the most importance, usually the subject and the verb.

- Nouns, pronouns, and verbs are the main actors in our grammar drama. The other parts of speech usually play a supporting role. They serve to tell us more about the simple clause.

- The use of a system for grammatically deconstructing the meaning of a sentence moves comprehension from a random guessing game of *gist* to a deliberate and structural unveiling of both literal and figurative comprehension.

Reading Comprehension Connection

A good percentage of secondary-age English learners grew up in what could be called the *gist era* of reading instruction and comprehension. Though never officially recognized as such, by the mid 1980s, many states advocated a reading theory that came largely from the field of psycholinguistics. Among other tenets, scholars emphasized that the brain was a prediction machine that seeks out patterns that it uses in turn to form complex hypotheses about language. Their reasoning came across as a call to abandon direct instruction of reading and writing and to instead immerse students in a "language-rich" environment in which their predicting, pattern-forming, hypothesis-generating brains would "come to know" language in all its forms (listening, speaking, reading, and writing). Whole language came to be the watchword, and teachers sat through trainings about what it meant to be a whole language teacher.

Whole language was touted as not only good for native English speakers, but it was also a veritable master key for English learners who would surely thrive in an environment staffed by a teacher who "was" whole language, and a classroom full of big books, chart paper, and listening stations and punctuated daily by extended—and sometimes dramatically presented—read-alouds. English learners were "taught" to read by making bold predictions based on pictures, to guess wildly at unknown words, and most of all, to not worry too much about skipping words and not getting quite the literal meaning of the sentence; gist was sufficient for now.

What these students—English-only and English learners alike—did not receive in many cases was instruction that showed them how grammar is used to make meaningful sentences, paragraphs, essays, books, speeches, and soliloquies. Few were the lessons on how to identify the subject of the sentence by looking for nouns and pronouns linked to action words. Lessons about how authors use grammar and its parts of speech to create a sense of time (*prepositions*), use verbs to reflect intent (*could, would, should*), or select just the right subordinating conjunction to make syntheses (*therefore, as a result*) were replaced instead with exhortations to "play with the language," "immerse yourself in language's beauty," and to "see in your mind what the author is conveying." Word-by-word analyses of text were far less frequent than were Venn diagrams showing similarities between stories. The teaching of word order rules went out the window, replaced by supercilious advice that sounded like, "Just skip those words," and "We'll figure that out later."

Academic Writing Connection

If one goes ballroom dancing armed with only two or three moves, one must repeat those moves over and over until the night is ended—or avoid dancing altogether. And so it is with too many secondary students' writing. They have a few simple sentence patterns that they use over and over again until reaching an end to the essay—sooner rather than later. Here is an example that could be proxy for thousands of other similar pieces of work.

Prompt: Describe the qualities of a good teacher and why you think those qualities are important.

Student Response: (Eighth grade intermediate English level)

My favorite teacher is Mrs. S because she is a good teacher for me and all students. Mrs. S teaches all the students in the class. She gives examples because all students in the class need help with math. She stay late after class to help the students. Another teacher that is a favorite teacher is Mr. B because he is nice and fun.

Quickly, see if you can find the sentence patterns that dominate this writing. How many of these sentences would you characterize as having an academic tone or flavor? As we saw in a previous chapter, academic writing is about moving subjects to different locations in sentences, using conjunctions to create compound and complex sentences, and using the myriad opportunities presented by adjectives, adverbs, and prepositions to spice up the writing by telling us more about when, why, how, or where the action takes place. The *Text-cavation* method described in this chapter represents a new way of using grammar for students and perhaps for many teachers. Grab your grammar shovel and let's dig in.

Students need to have a set of steps for using their grammar knowledge to comprehend sentences and larger pieces of academic text.

Method

Text-cavation

Description

Students identify the main idea and details of a sentence by linking grammar and interrogatives (who, what, where, when, why, how) to text structure.

Purpose

Deriving comprehension from written text requires a multitude of discrete grammar skills working together. The task is made more difficult for English learners who have to not only understand the content of the reading, but also decipher a variety of sentence structures. Through the eyes of English learners, academic sentences can look like nothing more than a jumble of words. By using an inverse structure of that utilized in the *Four-Picture Story Frames* method, students learn a deliberate way of linking their knowledge of the eight parts of speech to text comprehension. When students can analyze and understand sentence formulas and their underlying language structures, their reading comprehension of text is substantially facilitated.

Materials Needed

- ☐ text for student use
- ☐ chart paper
- ☐ markers
- ☐ *Grammar Wall*

Teacher Skills

- ✓ familiarity with the *Grammar Wall*
- ✓ knowledge of how interrogative questions (who, what, where, etc.) link to specific parts of speech
- ✓ ability to identify the main clause and surrounding details of a sentence

Language Objective: We will identify the main clause in a sentence and the supporting details.

Steps

This method aims to teach students to independently identify the main idea (subject and verb) of the sentence as well as the details (where, when, how, why). Previous exposure to and use of the *Grammar Wall* is mandatory. Practice of methods such as *Verb Tense Study, Syntax Surgery,* and *Four-Picture Story Frames* assist students greatly in learning and practicing *Text-cavation.* The steps for this method are listed below and are fully explained thereafter.

Text-cavation - Steps at a Glance

Preparation

1. Select text that students will use for the method.

2. Select at least three sentences for guided practice and three-six more for group and independent practice.

3. Write guided practice sentences on chart paper.

4. Text-cavate all sentences *before lesson begins* for your lesson plan.

5. Ensure that your *Grammar Wall* has the interrogatives posted where they belong with sufficient example words under each.

Procedures

First Lesson

- ✓ Link interrogatives to parts of speech on the *Grammar Wall.*
- ✓ Identify main components of sentence (who + what) by using illustration and analogy.
- ✓ Directly instruct a sample sentence.

Subsequent lessons
1. Introduce text.

Guided Sentences
2. Students read first selected sentence.
3. Teacher leads students to identify the "What" of the sentence.
    a. Where is the conjugated verb?
    b. If it's a compound or complex sentence, there may be more than one.
4. Teacher leads students to identify the "Who" of the sentence.
    a. normally in front of the verb
    b. does action of verb
5. Teacher leads students to formulate questions from the "Who+What." Underline and label the answers if they are found.
    a. Where
    b. When
    c. Why
    d. How
6. Teacher leads students to label the syntax pattern.

Practice Sentences
7. Students work in groups to text-cavate more sentences.
8. Students work independently to text-cavate remaining sentences.

Discussion of Steps

Before the lesson begins

Step 1-Select the text for student use.

As the goal of this method is increased reading comprehension, academic text should be used for *Text-cavation*. Expository text is best. Try using:

- passages from textbooks
- segments of articles from periodicals
- text from online academic resources for students

Step 2-Select sentences to "text-cavate."

In each text, you should be able to identify at least ten sentences for *Text-cavation*. Look for sentences that have some detail and don't only answer the questions, "who" and "what." Make sure that sentences you will ask students to "text-cavate" independently or in groups are only as difficult as sentences that you have practiced together.

Select at least three sentences for:

1. guided practice
2. group practice
3. independent practice

> **Tip!**
> Select sentences for guided practice that pose a new or challenging grammatical structure or concept for students.

Step 3- Write the guided practice sentences on chart paper.

Write each of the three guided practice sentences on chart paper leaving enough room for labeling and the syntax pattern.

Step 4- Complete the lesson plan by text-cavating sentences.

It's crucial that the teacher knows how to "text-cavate" each sentence before presenting the lesson to students. The following illustration and explanation will help you to understand how sentences are organized.

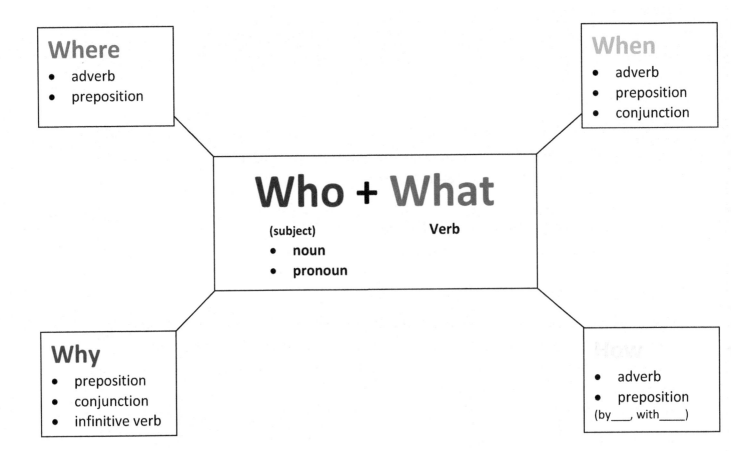

Clues to introduce new sentence/clause/idea:

- o a period (.)
- o a semi-colon (;)
- o coordinating conjunctions (for, and, nor, but, or, yet so).

*When any of the above is present, there may be more than one idea to "text-cavate."

At the center of every sentence is the subject and verb telling who and what. Every other question, where, when, why, and how is used to provide detail about the who and what. Understanding this makeup helps students not only to find the main idea of the sentence, but also to understand how the details support that main idea.

In completing the lesson plan, follow the same steps for *Text-cavation* that you will use with students. Use the following lesson plan sample and template to design your own lesson.

Guided Practice Sentences

Sentence 1:

After climbing around a flower, the bee carries pollen from the flower to its hive to feed the young.

Pattern: **When + Who + What + Where + Why**

Questions	Answers
1. What is the what, or the verb, in the sentence?	1. The what/verb is "carries (+pollen)."
2. What is the who, or the subject, in the sentence?	2. The who/subject is "the bee."
3. Where does the bee carry pollen?	3. The where is "from the flower to its hive."
4. When does the bee carry pollen?	4. The when is "after climbing around a flower."
5. How does the bee carry pollen?	5. (not stated)
6. Why does the bee carry pollen?	6. The why is "to feed the young."

Sentence 2:

In their hives, bees make honey from nectar so that they have something to eat when there are fewer flowers around.

Pattern: **Where + Who + What + How + Why**

Questions	Answers
1. What is the what, or the verb, in the sentence?	1. The what/verb is "make (+honey)."
2. What is the who, or the subject, in the sentence?	2. The who/subject is "bees."
3. Where do bees make honey?	3. The where is "in their hives."
4. When do bees make honey?	4. (not stated)
5. How do bees make honey?	5. The how is "with nectar."
6. Why do bees make honey?	6. The why is "so that they have something to eat when there are fewer flowers around."

Sentence 3:

The bees spread the honey into the honeycomb ⟨and⟩ then they fan it with their wings to make it dry out.

Pattern: **Who + What + Where + AND + When + Who + What + How + Why**

Questions	Answers
1. What is the what, or the verb, in the *first* clause?	1. The what/verb is "spread (the honey)."
2. What is the who, or the subject in the first clause?	2. The who/subject is "the bees."
3. Where do the bees spread the honey?	3. The where is, "into the honeycomb."
4. What is the what, or the verb, in the *second* clause?	4. The what/verb is "fan (it=the honey)."
5. What is the who, or the subject, in the *second* clause?	5. The who/subject is "they (=the bees)."
6. When do the bees fan the honey?	6. The when is, "then."
7. How do the bees fan the honey?	7. The how is, "with their wings."
8. Why do the bees fan the honey?	8. The why is, "to make it dry out."

243

Group Practice Sentences

Sentences	Pattern
Once most of the water is gone, the nectar becomes honey.	When + Who + What.
They mix the pollen with a bit of nectar to make it sticky, and then they pack it into the pollen basket.	Who + What + How + Why AND When + Who + What + Where.
When the bee rubs over the flower, the pollen gets caught in the hairs, and the bee can carry it back to its hive.	When + Who + What + Where AND Who + What + Where.

Independent Practice Sentences

Sentences	Pattern
Many bees have hairs on their legs or tummies to collect pollen.	Who + What + Where + Why.
Inside the honey stomach, the nectar is carried back to the hive, where it will be given to another bee.	Where + Who + What + Where.
So that it can be easily eaten by the bees later, the nectar is broken down by enzymes in the bee's mouth, before it is spread into the honeycomb.	Why + Who + What + How + Where + When.

Notes:

Guided Practice Sentences

Sentence 1:

Pattern:

Questions	Answers

Sentence 2:

Pattern:

Questions	Answers

Sentence 3:

Pattern:

Group Practice Sentences

Sentences	Pattern

Independent Practice Sentences

Sentences	Pattern

Notes:

Step 5-The prepared *Grammar Wall*

The interrogatives will not only help students to find the details in the sentence but will also show them a visual link between grammar and reading comprehension. The same interrogatives used in the *Four-Picture Story Frames* method and *Text-cavation* should also be posted on the *Grammar Wall* near the parts of speech that answer them. The following illustration shows the link between the parts of speech and the interrogatives they answer.

Adjectives *Who* (used to describe nouns and pronouns)	Nouns (subject) *Who*	Pronouns (subject) *Who*	Verbs *What*
Adverbs *How* of manner *Where* *When* of direction of time/ frequency	Prepositions *Why* of purpose *Where* *When* of location of time	Conjunctions *When* *Why* of time of cause	Interjections *Wow!*

Text-cavation

During the Lesson

For the first lesson

    ✓ <u>Link interrogatives to parts of speech on the *Grammar Wall.*</u>

In order to familiarize students with the use of the interrogatives on the *Grammar Wall,* review which parts of speech answer which questions. Consider building the diagram showing the who and what at the center with students (p. 241).

    ✓ <u>Identify the main components of a sentence.</u>

Students must understand that the simple clause of any sentence is the subject plus the verb (and the direct object if there is one). The only two questions that must be answered to form complete sentences are "Who?" and "What?"

Go back to the diagram with the who and the what at the center and help students to see that the other details revolve around the center of the sentence, telling more about it. Think of analogies for the components of the sentence to help students understand.

Tip!

Analogies for Sentence Structure

Consider using an analogy to help students understand the importance of the simple clause (the who and the what) within the sentence. The following are examples:

The who and the what are the sun and the other details are the planets revolving around them.

The who and the what are the brain telling the other details, or body parts, what to do.

The who and the what are the chassis of a car upon which all other parts are bolted.

Try your own!

    ✓ <u>Directly instruct a sample sentence.</u>

Before starting with the guided practice, lead students through a sample sentence in which you show them how you text-cavate a sentence using the interrogatives from the *Grammar Wall.*

Step 1- Introduce text.

Each student will need access to a copy of the text whether it is printed out or read from a book. Direct students to the text, but this is not the time to read the entire passage. *Text-cavation* works best when students have already read the passage once, before the lesson.

Explain to students that they will be practicing reading comprehension by identifying the simple clause and details of each sentence.

Tip!
How much do I box/underline?
Underline and box the entire phrase. In the sample below, the verb has been boxed, but the direct object (pollen) is only underlined to show that it's not the verb, but it *must* go with the verb.

Similarly, you can box the simple subject but underline the complete subject. You want to show students the complete parts of the sentence but also assure that the essential components stand out.

Guided Sentences

Step 2- Students read first selected sentence.

Step 3- Identify the "what" of the sentence.

Ask students to identify the what, or the verb, in the sentence. The verb will be conjugated, not in infinitive form, and usually follows the subject showing what the subject does. Once the "what" has been correctly identified, draw a circle or box around it and label it so that it stands apart from the rest of the sentence.

Step 4- Identify the "who" of the sentence.

Ask students to identify the who, or the subject in the sentence. The subject is a noun, pronoun, or noun phrase that usually comes before the verb either showing who/what does the action of the verb or who/what is being connected to a complement (adjective, other noun/pronoun, prepositional phrase) by the verb. Draw a circle or box around the subject and label it so that it also stands apart from the rest of the sentence.

The chart should now look like this.

Who   What
After climbing around a flower, the bee carries pollen from the flower to its hive to feed the young.

Step 5- Formulate detail questions from the who and the what.

Now that students have found the who and the what, they can form questions with the who and the what as the base by adding the interrogatives to the beginning. Make sure that students use the same verb tense as the sentence and ask the question **before** trying to identify the components of the sentence.

For instance, in our example from the previous page, the sentence is in the simple present. We can form new questions by using the base of the subject plus the verb: the bee carries pollen. Now attach the interrogatives to each.

_____ does the bee carry pollen?

(Insert interrogative.)

Working your way through the interrogatives, ask the four detail questions:

Where does the bee carry pollen?

When does the bee carry pollen?

How does the bee carry pollen?

Why does the bee carry pollen?

Tip!
Expository text is often written in simple past or simple present. If students have difficulty forming questions in either tense, refer them to the interrogative formula (found on the Preview Chart of a *Verb Tense Study)* for the appropriate verb tense.

Have students practice the question in pairs and then try to identify which part of the sentence answers the question, responding, "The where is _____." As a challenge ask students how they know that a component of the sentence is answered. Students should be able to use their knowledge of the *Grammar Wall* to answer this question. For example, "I know that 'after climbing around a flower' is a when because it begins with a preposition of time."

As each question is answered, underline and label the parts of the sentence with the students.

<u>Step 6- Label the syntax pattern.</u>

Ask students to identify the syntax pattern of the sentence. Write it below the sentence.

The chart should now look like this.

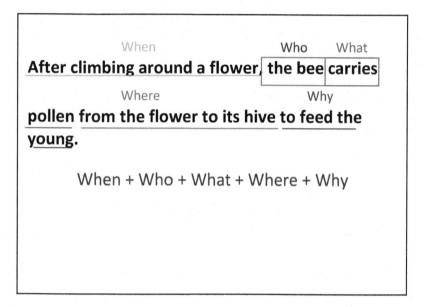

<u>Step 7- Group practice</u>

Students text-cavate at least three sentences following the same procedures as above in groups. Please review and correct the group work before allowing students to practice independently.

<u>Step 8-Independent practice</u>

Students independently text-cavate at least three sentences following the same procedures as above. This is an appropriate step to assign as homework.

Assessment

Student proficiency for "text-cavating" a passage can be assessed in the following ways:

- ✓ Students independently "text-cavate" a sentence from a published passage.
- ✓ Students "text-cavate" each other's sentences.
- ✓ Students generate the questions that should be asked for a sample sentence.
- ✓ Students produce their own sentence following the same syntax pattern as a recently "text-cavated" sentence.
- ✓ Students identify the main idea of a text after "text-cavating" many sentences from the passage.

What *Text-cavation* looks like across the language levels

Text-cavation can be completed with any language level. However, there are several components that will vary depending on student proficiency.

component/level	Beginner	Intermediate	Advanced
number of components/sentence	-two-four	-three-five	-four or more
types of sentence to "text-cavate"	-simple	-simple and complex	-all types
length of sentence	5-10 words	10-15 words	15+ words

What this Method _Isn't_

It's <u>not</u> a guessing game. Many students will be tempted to start at the beginning of the sentence and identify the parts of the sentence as they come upon them. This is very difficult. Have students find the simple clause **first** and then ask the interrogatives.

It's <u>not</u> the time to introduce a new grammar concept or verb tense. Students should be applying tenses and grammar concepts that they have _already_ learned for this method.

It's <u>not</u> independent reading. Students need guidance in seeing how sentences are organized. Showing them how to unearth the main idea and details in text is a skill that will assist them to increase their reading comprehension during independent reading at a later time.

Things to Re-think

1. How many times during their schooling have secondary English learners been told to "Find the main idea," or, "Add more details." Do you believe that in the absence of grammar knowledge on the part of a student, such exhortations mean anything at all?
2. The usual prescription for struggling secondary English learners is to give them lower-level reading materials. But if a student can't find the main idea and understand what kind of details may present themselves in a text, isn't such a simplistic approach silly?
3. What would you tell an English learner student who asks you why the _Text-cavation_ approach to comprehending text was not taught earlier –as in years earlier?

What to Expect

➢ As discussed earlier in this chapter, many English learners are used to understanding their reading at

---

Administrators' Corner

<u>What to look for in _Text-cavation_</u>

➔ Is the method clearly labeled?

➔ Are there at least three sentences on chart paper to be "text-cavated?"

➔ Is the _Grammar Wall_ labeled with the interrogatives?

➔ Are there sufficient words on the _Grammar Wall_ (at least 100) and under each interrogative for students to use?

➔ Is the syntax pattern written below each sentence?

➔ Do students find the simple clause (the who and the what) before finding anything else?

➔ Do students orally produce the questions with the simple clause as a base _before_ identifying the components of the sentence?

➔ Do students know the steps to _Text-cavation_ well enough that they can "text-cavate" sentences on their own or in groups?

a *gist* level. The results of this method are bittersweet for them: they recognize what they had been missing by way of details, yet now have to work a bit harder to exhume those details.

➢ You may find *Text-cavating* to be a bit of a challenge yourself. If you are a native or highly proficient English user, breaking the text down may seem bulky at first. Your own sense of what sounds right could also get in the way. Start with easy sentences.

➢ On a related note, learning how to speak in *Text-cavationese* takes some learning for most teachers. As you text-cavate out loud with your students, you will begin using a very sophisticated lexicon to describe what you are doing. Don't get frustrated.

➢ Don't lose the meaning of the text in the service of an end-of-the-world *Text-cavation*. In other words, remember that the process of text-cavating is in service to comprehension. The end goal is for students to understand, not to have bloodied the text with arrows, boxes, and grammar formulas with no idea of what the words actually convey.

➢ You should see a parallel increase in complexity of students' writing as a result of regular text-cavating. And why not? Their analyses of how academic writers craft text helps to better inform authors setting out to write good text. A win-win situation for all.

➢ Looking for a good method that ties directly to state-mandated tests of reading? By now you have probably seen the value of *Text-cavation* for helping students to answer reading test questions.

Voices from the Classroom

This method is a complete shift in perspective on reading comprehension. As a reading teacher, I have always been focused teaching my students the basic skills of identifying main idea and details, making inferences and using context clues to access the meaning of the text. While I still do that, this method is a great one to use before any of the above skills are practiced because it asks students to really focus on the meaning sentence by sentence from a grammar perspective.

I have found this method so effective that I trained my English Only students to use it when they face challenging text. I find this method gets more challenging to use as the text get higher in lexile and the syntax gets more complicated. However, it still forces a critical eye on what we are reading. My advice when starting this method is to keep it simple with sentences that have obvious interrogatives so students are successful. –Danielle from Newark, CA

Final Thoughts

What we have tried to do in this book is to weave together, in a single tapestry, information from three different areas: history, linguistics, and methodology. By showing the teleological relationship between history and linguistics, we wanted to show how language teaching and learning have not been immune or insulated from social, cultural, and academic factors of the day. It is true of many fields that, as the world turns, so too do the thinking and actions of those working in a certain discipline.

A central point of the book was to demonstrate clearly how philosophy and ideology impact teacher behavior, both at a conscious and unconscious level. Whatever the case, changes in teacher behavior have short- and long-term implications for the students in classrooms. That so many adolescent English learners lack basic grammar knowledge and application skills shows the dynamic impact of teacher behavior as derived from philosophy. In short, we attempted to show through student voices, analogies, and metaphors that we indeed reap what we sow. This book is our attempt to change the philosophy and methods of our sowing, or to at least bring them to light to allow for more conscious choice-making in our instruction of English learners.

Certainly, many of the ideas advanced in this book will be met with rejection, argument, and possibly derision. Old paradigms die hard, and a *New View* that rejects a previously simple, easy view of language learning is likely to take some punches. Our passionate defense of informed, planned, deliberate, challenging and frequently enjoyable grammar teaching and learning is also likely to invoke the enmity and disdain of those who believe language to be acquired naturally through simple social interaction over time. But we and other educators with whom we have worked during the past 25 years around the country and abroad agree that providing direct grammar-based language instruction to English learners is the best chance we have of helping them to read with comprehension and to write academically at grade level. No one in this camp claims that it is or will be easy, but we stand resolute in believing that this *New View* is the only way to open the world of literacy and true education to the thousands of students sitting in classrooms today who know that they need to be taught the English language.

Bibliography

Ackrill, J.L. (Edd.). (1988). A New Aristotle Reader. NJ: Princeton University Press.

August, D.; Carlo, M.; Dressler, C. & Snow, C. (2005). The critical role of vocabulary development for English language learners. *Learning Disabilities Research Practice, 20,* 50-57.

August, D., & Hakuta, K. (1997). *Improving schooling for language-minority students.* Washington, DC: National Academy Press.

Bailey, N., Madden, C., & Krashen, S.D. (1974) Is there a "natural sequence" in adult second language learning? *Language Learning, 24,* 235-243.

Beck, I. L., McKeown, M. G., & Kucan, L. (2002) *Bringing words to life: Robust vocabulary instruction; solving problems in teaching of literacy.* New York: Guilford.

Berliner, D. C. (1984). The half-full glass: A review of research on teaching. In P. L. Hosford (Ed.), Using what we know about teaching (pp. 51-77), Alexandria, VA: Association for Supervision and Curriculum Development.

Bloom, B. S. (1974). Time and learning. *American Psychology, 29,* 682-688.

Borg, W. R. (1980). Time and school learning. In C. Denham & A. Lieberman (Eds.), Time to learn (pp. 33-72). Washington, DC: U.S. Department of Education, National Institute of Education.

Brown, R. (1973). *A first language.* Cambridge, MA: Harvard University Press.

Bruck, M., & Genesee, G. (1995). Phonological awareness in young second language learners. *Journal of child Language, 22,* 307-324.

Cameron, J., & Clark, K. (2011) *The Painless, Plan-Less Grammar Guide.* Sacramento, CA: Innovative Grammar

Capie, W., & Tobin, K. (1981). Pupil engagement in learning tasks: A fertile area for research in science teaching. *Journal of Research in Science Teaching, 18*(5), 409-417.

Carroll, J. B. (1963). A model of school learning. *Teachers College Record, 64*, 723-733.

Catts, H. W., Fey, M. E., Zhang, X., & Tomblin, J. B. (1999). Language basis of reading and reading disabilities: Evidence from a longitudinal investigation. *Scientific Studies of Reading, 3*, 331-361.

Catts, H., Hogan, T., & Adolf, S. (2005). Developmental changes in reading and reading disabilities. In H. W. Catts & A. G. Kamhi (Eds.), *The connections between language and reading disabilities* (pp. 25-40). Mahwah, NJ: Erlbaum.

Chiape, P., & Siegel, L. S. (1999). Phonological awareness and reading acquisition in English- and Punjabi-speaking Canadian children. *Journal of Educational Psychology, 91*, 20-28.

Chiape, P., & Siegel, L. S. (2006). A longitudinal study of reading development of Canadian Children from Diverse linguistic backgrounds. *Elementary School Journal, 107*, 135-152.

Chiape, P., & Siegel, L. S., & Gottardo, A. (2002). Reading-related skills of kindergartners from diverse linguistic backgrounds. *Applied Psycholinguistic, 23*, 95-116.

Clark, K. (in press). *Accelerating Language Development: New Views and New Results.* Phoenix, AZ: CCT Educational Publications.

Cisero, C., & Royer, J. (1995). The development and cross-language transfer of phonological awareness. *Contemporary Educational Psychology, 20*, 275-303.

Couper, G. (2006). The short and long-term effects of pronunciation instruction. *Prospect, 21,* (46-66).

Cummins, James. "The Role of Primary Language Development in Promoting Educational Success for Language Minority Students," *Schooling and Language Minority Students: A Theoretical Framework* . Los Angeles, California: Evaluation, Dissemination and Assessment Center, California State University, Los Angeles, 1981.

DeKeyser, R. M. (2000). The robustness of critical period effects in second language acquisition. *Studies in Second Language Acquisition, 22,*499-533.

Derwing, T. M., Munro, M. J., & Wiebe, G. (1998). Evidence in Favor of a Broad Framework for Pronunciation Instruction. *Language Learning, 48,* 393-410.

Dickinson, D. K., & Sprague, K. E. (2001). The nature and impact of early childhood care environments on the language and early literacy development of children from low-income families. In S. B. Neuman & D. K. Dickinson (Eds.), *Handbook of early literacy research* (pp. 263-280). New York: Guilford.

Dionysius Thrax, *Techne Grammatike (The Art of Grammar) c. 100 bc*

Dulay, H. C., & Burt, M. K. (1973). Should we teach children syntax? *Language Learning, 23,* 245-258.

Dulay, H. C., & Burt, M. K. (1974). Natural sequences in child second language acquisition. *Language Learning, 24,* 37-53.

Durgunoglu, A., Nagy, W., & Hancin-Bhatt, B. (1993). Cross-language transfer of phonological awareness. *Journal of Educational Psychology, 85,* 453-465.

Echevarria, J., Short, D., & Vogt, M. (2000). *Making Content Comprehensible for English Language Learners*. MA: Allyn & Bacon.

Ellis, N. (2002). Frequency effects in language processing: A review with implications for theories of implicit and explicit language acquisition. *Studies in Second Language Acquisition, 24,* 143-188.

Fisher, C. W., Berliner, D. C., Filby, N. N., Marliave, R., Cahen, L.S., & Dishaw, M. (1980). Teaching behaviors, academic learning time, and student achievement; An overview. In C. Denham & A. Lieberman (Eds.), *Time to learn* (pp. 7-32). Washington, DC: U.S. Department of Education, National Institute of Education.

Fitzgerald, J. (1995a). English-as-a-second language learners' cognitive reading processes: A review of research in the United States. *Review of Educational Research,* 65, 145-190.

Fotos, S., & Ellis, R. (1991). Communicating About Grammar: A Task-Based Approach. *Tesol Quarterly, 25* (4), 605-628.

Fries, C. 1952. *The Structure of English: An Introduction to the Construction of English Sentences. New York: Harcourt Brace.*

Genessee, F., Lindholm-Leary, K., Saunders, W., & Christian, D. (2004). *Educating English language learners: A synthesis of research evidence.* Santa Cruz, CA: Center for Research on Education, Diversity, and Excellence.

Gersten, R., & Baker, S. (2000a). The professional knowledge base on instructional practices that support cognitive growth for English-language learners. In R. Gersten, E. Schiller, & S. Vaughn (Eds.), *Contemporary special education research: Syntheses of the knowledge base on critical instructional issues* (pp. 31-79). Mahwah, NJ: Erlbaum.

Gersten, R., & Baker, S. (2000b). What we know about effective instructional practices for English-language learners. *Exceptional Children*, 66, 454-470.

Geva, E., Yaghoub-Zadeh, Z., & Schuster, B. (2000). Understanding individual differences in word recognition skills of ESL children. *Annuals of Dyslexia*, 50, 123-154.

Giovannone, C. (2011). Arizona SEI Program: Presentation to the ELL Task Force. Unpublished manuscript, Arizona Department of Education, Phoenix, AZ.

Goldschneider, J. M., & DeKeyser, R. M. (2005). Explaining the "Natural Order of L2 Morpheme Acquisition" in English: A Meta-analysis of Multiple Determinants. *Language Learning, 55,* 27-77.

Gottardo, A., Stanorvish, K. E., & Siegel, L. S. (1996). The relationships between phonological sensitivity, syntactic processing, and verbal working memory in the reading performance of third-grade children. *Journal of Experimental Child Psychology, 63,* 563-582.

Hoover, W. A., & Gough, P. B. (1990). The simple view of reading. *Reading and Writing: An Interdisciplinary Journal,* 2, 127-160.

Johnson, J. S., & Newport, E. L. (1989). Critical period effects in second language learning: The influence of maturational state on the acquisition of English as a second language. *Cognitive Psychology, 20,* 60-99.

Karweit, N. "Time-on-Task: A Research Review" Report No 332 Baltimore Center for Social Organization of Schools, The Johns Hopkins University, January 1983.

Klein, W., & Dittmar, N. (1979). *Developing grammars.* Berlin: Springer.

Krashen, S. D., & Pon, P., (1975). An error analysis of and advanced ESL learner. *Working Papers in Bilingualism, 7,* 125-129.

Krashen, Stephen D. "Bilingual Education and Second Language Acquisition Theory," *Schooling and Language Minority Students: A Theoretical Framework* . Los Angeles, California: Evaluation, Dissemination and Assessment Center, California State University, Los Angeles, 1981.

Krashen, S.D. (1982) *Principles and practice in second language acquisition*. Oxford: Pergamon.

Larsen-Freeman, D.E. (1976). An explanation for the morpheme acquisition order of second language learners. *Language Learning, 26*, 125-134.

Larsen-Freeman, D.E., & Long, M. H. (1991). *An introduction to second language acquisition research*. New York: Longman.

Lesaux, N. K., & Siegel, L. S. (2003). The development of reading in children who speak English as a second language. *Developmental Psychology, 39*, 1005-1019.

Mitchell, Rosamond (1994). "The communicative approach to language teaching". In Swarbick, Ann. *Teaching Modern Languages.* New York: Routledge. Pp. 33-42.

Mokhtari, K. & Thompson, H. B. (2006). How Problems of Reading Fluency and Comprehension Are Related to Difficulties in Syntactic Awareness Skills Among Fifth Graders. *Reading Research & Instruction, 46,* (73-94).

Mulroy, D. (2003). *The War Against Grammar*. Portsmouth, NH: Boynton/Cook.

Munro, M. J., & Derwing, T. M. (1994). Evaluations of foreign accent in extemporaneous and read material. *Language Testing, 11*, 253-266.

Norris, J., & Ortega, L. (2000). Does type of instruction make a difference? Substantive findings from a meta-analytic review. *Language Learning* 51, Supplement 1: 157-213.

Perlmutter, M. (1989). Intelligibility rating of L2 speech pre- and postintervention. *Perceptual and Motor Skills, 68,* 515-521.

Pinker, S. (1994). *The Language Instinct: How the Mind Creates Language.* New York, NY: HarperCollins.

Rosenshine, B. (1980). How time is spent in elementary classrooms. In C. Denham & A. Lieberman (Eds.), Time to learn (pp. 107-126). Washington, DC: U.S. Department of Education, National Institute of Education.

Santa Cruz, A., personal communication, July 17, 2010.

Saunders, W., Foorman, B., & Carlson, C. (2006). Is a Separate Block of Time for Oral English Language Development in Programs for English Learners Needed? *Elementary School Journal, 107(2), 181-198.*

Siegel, L. S. (1993). The development of reading. In H. W. Reese (Ed.), *Advances in child development and behavior* (vol. 24, pp. 63-97). San Diego: Academic Press.

Siegel, L. S., & Ryan, E. B. (1998). Development of grammatical sensitivity, phonological, and short-term memory skills in normally achieving and learning disabled children. *Developmental Psychology,* 24, 28-37.

Spada, N., & Lightbown, P. (1993). Instruction and the development of questions in the L2classroom. *Studies in Second Language Acquisition* 15 (2): 205-221.

Swanson, H. L., Sáez, L., Gerber, M., & Leafstedt, J. (2004). Literacy and cognitive functioning in bilingual and nonbilingual children at or not at risk for reading disabilities. *Journal of Educational Psychology, 96*, 3-18.

Taraban, R. (2004). Drawing learners' attention to syntactic context aids gender-like category induction. *Journal of Memory and Language, 51*, 202-216.

Tarone, E. E. (1985). Variability in interlanguage use: A study of style-shifting in morphology and syntax. *Language Learning, 35*, 373-404.

Terrell, Tracy D. "A Natural Approach to Second Language Acquisition and Learning," *Modern Language Journal*, XLI, No. 7 (November, 1977), 325-337.

Terrell, Tracy D. "The Natural Approach in Bilingual Education," ," *Schooling and Language Minority Students: A Theoretical Framework* . Los Angeles, California: Evaluation, Dissemination and Assessment Center, California State University, Los Angeles, 1981.

Tunmer, W. E., & Hoover, W. (1992). Cognitive and linguistic factors in learning to read. In P. B. Gough, L. C. Ehri, & R. Treiman (Eds.), *Reading acquisition* (pp. 175-214). Hillsdale, NJ: Erlbaum.

Ulanoff, S. H., & Pucci, S. L. (1999). Learning words from books: The effects of read-aloud on second-language acquisition. *Bilingual Research Journal,* 23, 409-422.

Verhoeven, L. (1994). Transfer in bilingual development: The linguistic interdependence hypothesis revisited. *Language Learning,* 44, 381-415.

Vygotsky, L.S. (1978). *Mind in society: The development of higher psycholigical processes.* Cambridge, Mass.: Harvard University Press.

Walberg, H. I. 1989c. "Productive Teaching and Instruction: Assessing the Knowledge Base." *Kappan*, in press.

CPSIA information can be obtained
at www.ICGtesting.com
Printed in the USA
BVOW07s1808160817
492229BV00008B/21/P

9 780983 899013